# A2 in a Week

D1076892

## Psychology

David
Abbey College,
Birmingham/Manchester
Series Editor: Kevin Byrne

Where to find

How To Use this book                         3

Social Psychology                            4

Physiological Psychology                     14

Classification and
Psychopathology                              22

Therapeutic Approaches                       34

Criminological Psychology                    44

Health Psychology                            54

Statistics and Research Methods              64

Perspectives, Debates and Ethics             72

Exam Practice Questions                      83

Use your Knowledge Answers                   85

Letts Educational
4 Grosvenor Place, London SW1X 7DL
School enquiries: 01539 564910
Parent & student enquiries: 01539 564913
E-mail: mail@lettsed.co.uk

Website: www.letts-educational.com

First published 2001
10 9 8 7 6 5

**British Library Cataloguing in Publication Data**
A CIP record for this book is available from the British Library.

ISBN 978-1-84315-818-9

Cover design by Purple, London

Prepared by *specialist* publishing services, Milton Keynes

Printed in Dubai

# How To Use This Book

The following chart shows which chapters are relevant to the specification that you are studying.

| | AQA-A | AQA-B | OCR | Edexcel |
|---|:---:|:---:|:---:|:---:|
| **Chapter 1**<br>Social psychology | ✔ | ✔ | | |
| **Chapter 2**<br>Physiological psychology | ✔ | | | |
| **Chapter 3**<br>Classification and psychopathology | ✔ | ✔ | | ✔ |
| **Chapter 4**<br>Therapeutic approaches | ✔ | ✔ | | ✔ |
| **Chapter 5**<br>Criminological psychology | | ✔ | ✔ | ✔ |
| **Chapter 6**<br>Health psychology | | ✔ | ✔ | ✔ |
| **Chapter 7**<br>Statistics and research methods | ✔ | ✔ | ✔ | ✔ |
| **Chapter 8**<br>Perspectives, debates and ethics | ✔ | ✔ | ✔ | ✔ |

This book does not attempt to provide comprehensive coverage of the A2 psychology specifications, but has topics which are relevant to as many of the different specifications as possible. These have been carefully chosen, with the actual examinations in mind, to provide enough coverage and choice.

Do not ignore chapters whose titles are not relevant to your specification, as they may contain some information which is relevant to your specification. For example, if you are studying health psychology for the OCR or Edexcel specifications, there is much relevant material in the chapter on physiological psychology.

# Social Psychology

## Test your knowledge

**1** According to the social-learning theory, children may _____ aggression from a behavioural _____ .

**2** One situational determinant of bystander behaviour is that when more people are present, we are _____ likely to help.

**3** According to the _____ hypothesis, bystander behaviour is motivated by a desire to help the victim.

**4** Lab studies tend to show that children who watch aggressive TV are _____ likely to be aggressive themselves, but such studies may lack _____ validity.

**5** According to the matching hypothesis of interpersonal attraction, we tend to have partners who have a _____ level of attractiveness to ourselves.

**6** According to the need-satisfaction theory, we choose partners who can _____ our needs.

**7** According to the social-exchange theory, when _____ outweigh _____ , we are likely to end that relationship.

**8** In collectivist cultures, the _____ marriage is more common than in individualist cultures.

## Answers

 **If you got them all right, skip to page 13**

**30 minutes**

# Improve your knowledge

| Key points from AS | AS in a Week reference |
|---|---|
| Methods and assumptions of the social approach | page 12 |
| Conformity and obedience | pages 12–14 |
| Theories and studies into the origins of prejudice | pages 14–15 |

Two social-psychological theories which have considered the cause of aggression are the frustration-aggression hypothesis and the social learning theory. According to the frustration-aggression hypothesis, if an individual is thwarted on the way to a goal, the resulting frustration will increase the probability of an aggressive response. Support for this idea comes from a study by Barker *et al* (1941). Young children were frustrated by being shown a room full of attractive toys, which were kept out of reach. After a long wait, the children were finally allowed to play with them. The frustrated group were extremely destructive, tending to smash, throw and stand on toys rather than play, when compared to a non-frustrated group. An important distinction is between frustration and deprivation. The Barker *et al* study shows that children without toys do not necessarily aggress. It was those children who expected to play with the toys who experienced frustration when thwarted. The same principle operates on a societal level. The most serious riots do not occur in the areas of greatest poverty, but in areas where, for a minority group, things are bad compared to the majority. It is this relative deprivation that introduces socio-economic factors (e.g. housing, education, welfare, etc.) to aggression.

Many factors can induce aggression in a person suffering little frustration, or inhibit an aggressive response in a person frustrated. These factors are the product of social learning. Support for this theory comes from a study by Bandura *et al* (1963). Children watched a film where an adult kicking and punching a bobo doll was either punished or rewarded. After the film, the children were allowed to enter one by one a playroom that contained many toys which had been seen in the film, including a bobo doll. They were left for ten minutes and their behaviour observed for aggressive content by trained raters. As expected, the children who watched the adult model being rewarded were more aggressive than those who had seen the model punished. However, a later test showed no differences between these groups; they were both aggressive. Bandura has been criticised for not specifying which role models are likely to be imitated. Critics also suggested that it was not ethically correct to expose young children to aggressive media.

Research has identified a number of environmental stressors that influence aggressive behaviour, including temperature, noise and crowding. With regard to temperature, field studies have suggested that violent crime increases in the hotter months and decreases in the cooler months. However, this might just be a result of more people coming into contact with each other, as more people tend to spend more time outdoors in hot weather. Lab studies suggest that aggression reaches a maximum at moderate temperatures (Halpern, 1995). As temperature increases, participants (pps) become more aggressive, but as it continues to increase, pps become more concerned at escaping. Research has shown that as levels of noise increase, so do levels of aggression, perhaps as a result of arousal or stress. In one study, pps solving maths problems were exposed to unpredictable noise (Donnerstein & Wilson, 1976). One group had no control, but the other believed they could stop the noise at any point. When pps could give shocks to someone who had angered them, those from the no control condition showed more aggression. So noise only appears to affect aggression when we cannot control it. Generally, research into crowding has been inconclusive. Stokols et al (1973) found that men rated themselves as more aggressive in a small room with eight people than when in a large room with eight people. However, women did not, and other studies have replicated this gender difference.

**2** Research has looked at why some people help in emergency situations (bystander intervention) and why some people do not (bystander apathy). Darley & Latané (1968) suggested that the apathy was a result of many people being present at the scene but no one person taking responsibility for taking action (this was termed a diffusion of responsibility). They tested this hypothesis with an experiment. Pps were placed in different rooms and allowed to communicate via intercom. An epileptic seizure was simulated by an accomplice. Pps were allocated to one of three groups. In group A the pp was the only bystander. Group B pps were one of two bystanders and Group C pps were one of five bystanders. When pps were alone they were more likely to offer help and were quicker to do so than when they believed there were a number of pps. As the number of bystanders increased, pps were less likely to offer help and took longer. Piliavin *et al* (1981) highlighted some confusion between the terms diffusion of responsibility, where responsibility is accepted by the pp but shared between all witnesses, and dissolution of responsibility, when the behaviour of other bystanders cannot be observed and the pp 'rationalises' that someone else must have already intervened.

Latané & Rodin (1970) investigated some of the other situational determinants of bystander behaviour. A female experimenter asked college students to fill out a questionnaire. The experimenter retired to the next room and staged an accident (a tape recording of a person falling off a chair, screaming and crashing to the floor). When pps were alone, 70 per cent offered help, but when pps were paired with an accomplice who acted as if nothing had happened, only 20 per cent offered help. When subsequently interviewed, the unhelpful pps had concluded that the accident wasn't serious partly because of the inactivity of their partner. According to Latané & Nida (1981) non-intervention becomes an act of conformity. For the individual, others were defining the reasonableness and appropriateness of helping or not helping. Taking cues from others can be misleading in critical situations and we may conclude that it is inappropriate to intervene.

**3** Two social-psychological theories to explain the behaviour of people in emergency situations are the negative state relief model and the empathy-altruism hypothesis. According to the empathy-altruism hypothesis (Bateson & Oleson, 1991), bystander behaviour is motivated by the desire to help the victim. Empathy includes feeling sympathetic and compassionate towards the victim. Support for the idea comes from Smith (1992) who showed that emergency situations that increase empathy result in more helping behaviour and vice versa. In an experimental situation, pps watched an accomplice receiving electric shocks. Empathy was manipulated by telling pps they were either very similar (high empathy) or dissimilar (low empathy) to the accomplice. In the high empathy condition, pps tried to help the accomplice by stopping the experiment or offering to change places. In the low empathy condition, pps were less likely to offer help. A critic of this hypothesis was Archer (1984) who suggested the helping behaviour was not actually based on empathy but a desire to not appear as unhelpful to the experimenter.

According to the negative state relief model (Cialdini *et al*, 1981), bystander behaviour is motivated by a desire to reduce negative feelings caused by seeing someone in distress. Support for this model comes from a study by Cialdini *et al* (1987), who showed that when empathy occurred, sadness also occurred. Helping behaviour increased when sadness increased, but not when empathy increased, suggesting that the important factor was the negative feelings. However, people still help, even when they do not know if their sad feelings will be alleviated. One important cross-cultural comparison is between societies with individualistic cultures and societies with communal cultures. Nadler (1986) studied cultural differences within Israel and found that people living in communal societies (kibbutzim) expected to be dependent on one another and were thus willing to seek help when it was needed. In contrast, people living in the city placed a greater emphasis on self-reliance and were therefore reluctant to turn to others for help. Thus socialisation in different subcultures in Israel resulted in differences in help-seeking behaviour.

**4** Psychological research has considered the influence of the media on both pro- and anti-social behaviour. Bandura's laboratory experiments in the 1960s demonstrated that young children can imitate the aggressive behaviour of role models. This and evidence from other studies suggests that violence on television is potentially dangerous in that it serves as a model for behaviour in young children. These types of lab experiments have been criticised as artificial on the basis that results cannot be generalised to real-life circumstances. It is possible to overcome some of the problems of lab studies by using field experiments which have high ecological validity since they are carried out in real life settings using wider samples, but these studies also have flaws. Parke *et al* (1977) showed one group of boys living in a juvenile detention centre a violent film and showed a non-violent film to another group. The boys were assessed during and after the week when the film was shown. The boys who watched the violent film showed more aggression, both physical and verbal. However, since the two groups of boys already existed prior to the study it is possible that they were not equal. One group may already have been more violent than the other. Also, it would be difficult to generalise to all children from these results since the sample used young offenders who are not representative of all children. The conclusion from a large number of studies is that observing violence is no more than a contributory factor in aggressive behaviour.

Research has also questioned the effect of watching pro-social behaviour: do we imitate these helpful role models as well? A number of television programmes have been broadcast with the intention of enhancing the social maturity of their viewers. The most successful has been *Sesame Street*. The series was originally targeted at disadvantaged children living in urban ghettos in the U.S. to teach them a variety of social and mental skills that they would need at school. Its appeal is far more wide-reaching than could ever have been imagined, but does it actually achieve its aim of having a pro-social effect? The evidence seems to say it does. Research has shown that children as young as four to seven years old are able to identify and remember cooperative helping behaviours emphasised in certain segments of the show (Gunter & McAleer, 1990). Another programme, *Mr Rogers' Neighbourhood*, was also created to try and improve children's social awareness and social skills, and similar effects were found. Four-year-old children who were shown four episodes of the series depicting characters attempting to understand and help a stranger, were better able to behave in a helpful and cooperative way than children who watched different programmes (Coates & Pusser, 1975). Evidence seems to indicate that when young children watch standard TV programmes in which the main characters display concern and consideration for others, their own concern and consideration may also increase.

5 Interpersonal attraction is the study of our relationships with friends, family and partners. Research has shown that one of the most important factors in interpersonal attraction is physical attractiveness. According to the matching hypothesis, despite the fact that most of us would prefer an attractive partner, we tend to have partners who possess a similar level of attractiveness to ourselves. A study by Murstein (1972) supports this idea. Photographs of couples who had been dating for at least six months were rated for attractiveness by participants. Results showed that these couples were rated as similar in levels of attractiveness compared to random people paired as couples. Cunningham (1986) found that two facial types were thought to be the most attractive: the childlike face has widely spaced eyes and a small nose; and the mature face has high cheekbones, a large smile and large pupils. Langlois (1990) used computer-generated faces that were composites of many others and found the most average face was considered the most attractive.

**6** Two theories of relationship formation are the socio-biological theory and the reward theory. The socio-biological theory is based on the findings that in general men tend to prefer partners who are younger than themselves, whilst women select older partners. Kenrick & Keefe (1992) collected 'lonely hearts' advertisements and found that women of all ages advertised for older partners and men over the age of 40 advertised for younger partners. One explanation for these findings is that preferences reflect inherited reproductive strategies. Because men can reproduce throughout most of their adult lives they are attracted to women of child-bearing age. For a woman, reproductive success would be maximised by a male past the age of puberty who would be willing and able to stay around to help feed and protect his mate and their offspring. The hypothesis is that natural selection resulted in women attracted to strong men with adequate resources and abilities. This theory cannot account for childless couples and presumes heterosexuality and that sexual attraction is about reproduction. According to the need-satisfaction theory, we develop relationships with people who can fulfil our needs (Argyle, 1994). For example, some people have high affiliation needs, seeking company and approval, while others may have a high need for dominance, making all the decisions and being bossy. However, this model ignores relationships based on equity and fairness rather than reward. Some very strong family relationships are based on kinship bonds with very little reinforcement.

**7** Two theories that might explain how people maintain relationships and how relationships end (dissolution) are the social exchange theory and the equity theory. Thibaut & Kelley (1959) in the social exchange theory, proposed that we maintain our relationships on the basis of profits (what do I get out of the relationship?) and costs (what do I have to put into the relationship?). If the costs begin to outweigh the profits then the relationship is likely to end. Clark & Mills (1979) suggested that the exchange theory is only relevant for the type of couple concerned with 'score keeping' (the exchange couple) and not for the type of couple concerned with helping each other (the communal couple). According to the equity theory (Walster et al, 1978), it is not so much the actual profits or costs that are important, but how they balance out. Relationships are maintained as long as profits and costs balance (e.g. favours are 'paid back' with equivalent favours). In an unequitable relationship (e.g. favours are not 'paid back'), the most likely outcome is that the relationship will end, unless there is a chance of restoring equity. A study by Rusbult & Martz (1995) showed that the equity theory has problems explaining why someone would stay in an abusive relationship, because it does not take into account investment. When people are deciding whether to end a relationship, they do not just weigh up the benefits and costs, but also how much they have invested in the relationship.

Hendrick & Hendrick (1986) have proposed six different kinds of love: passionate, friendship, game-playing, possessive, logical and selfless love. Romantic partners tend to be similar in the kind of love they express, although males tend to be higher on passionate and game-playing love and females higher on friendship, logical and possessive love. Most psychological research has tended to focus on passionate love, which refers to the sudden, intense and all-consuming response to another person, with 'falling in love' often likened to an accident. Aron *et al* (1989) pointed out that people don't tend to 'fall in friendship' and that love is not determined by the same factors that lead to friendship but more on the desirable aspects of the other person. Hatfield (1988) identified some characteristics of passionate love: sexual attraction, physiological arousal, preoccupation with partner, despair at the thought of relationship ending and the need to be loved in return. Fisher (1992) proposed an evolutionary explanation for passionate love. As humans began to stand on hind legs, the most effective child-rearing strategy was a male-female bond. For this to work, the couple had to like and trust one another and so a brain chemistry developed to produce loving feelings. This proposition has resulted in some unusual research. Touflexis (1993) found that people in love produce neurochemicals which are related to happiness and excitement. Kellerman *et al* (1989) found that when two strangers look into each other's eyes for two minutes, they are likely to report feelings of passionate love.

**8** Moghaddam *et al* (1993) noted some cross-cultural differences in relationships. For example, Western relationships tend to be individualistic, voluntary and temporary, whereas relationships within some non-Western cultures are collective, obligatory and permanent. According to this distinction, the majority of research is only relevant to Western cultures. According to Hofstede (1994), individualist cultures place more emphasis on the needs of individuals, whereas in collectivist cultures, responsibility to the family or community is more important. The different values of these cultures can be seen in marriage and divorce. In the West, marriage is seen as a bond between two people based on love (although this may be changing) and divorce rates are high. In collectivist cultures, marriage is seen as a union between two families, arranged marriage is more common and divorce rates are much lower. Some research has considered how immigrant families have adapted to living in the West. Ghuman (1994) found that arranged marriages persisted for Sikhs, Hindus and Muslims living in Britain and Canada, although the practice was leading to conflict between the older and younger generations. Another study of Hindu couples living in Leicester found that only 8 per cent of the marriages were 'truly' arranged (Goodwin *et al*, 1997). In the majority of cases, partners had met at social events and were given the option of refusing their partner.

The majority of psychological research is based only on heterosexual relationships and so has ignored, and in some cases marginalised, the experiences of homosexual relationships. Gay and lesbian relationships are subject to different pressures, including the effect of growing up in a society where homosexual relationships are classified as unacceptable, the unequal age of consent for gay men and the way that few happy lesbian and gay relationships are presented by the media. These pressures create issues that are particular to gay and lesbian relationships, such as whether to make public their sexuality and how to recognise other gay people. Some gay people choose not to make their sexuality public through fear of rejection and physical abuse. If they keep their sexuality secret then family and friends may maintain unrealistic expectations of their developing heterosexual relationships and they may have no close confidantes to talk openly with. For this reason, some gay people choose to spend their social lives in the company of other gay people, although for others with families and children it is not an option. Another kind of understudied relationship is the electronic relationship. Electronic relationships refer to those using the Internet; e-mail, chat rooms and support groups are no less real than face-to-face relationships. A survey by America On-Line showed that the top ten chatrooms were all used for sexual relationships: three were for gay men, one for lesbians, five for heterosexuals and one for people interested in group sex and/or partner swapping. Electronic relationships differ from face-to-face relationships in that they offer an opportunity for deception – people can pretend to be who they want to be and act out fantasies which they could not enact in their ordinary relationships. Some people have a preference for electronic relationships even when given the opportunity to meet face-to-face (Reid, 1998). Indeed, some people who have chosen to meet have been extremely disappointed.

# Social Psychology

## Use your knowledge

**Hint**

**1** Evaluate the evidence for the social learning theory of aggression.

*ecological validity, short- or long-term findings*

**2** Do environmental stressors make us more aggressive?

*temperature, noise and crowding*

**3** What is the difference between the empathy-altruism and negative state relief models of bystander behaviour?

*selfish vs selfless motivation*

**4** Does the media have a pro-social effect?

*do children imitate pro-social behaviour?*

**5** What kind of faces do we find the most attractive?

*the matching hypothesis and composite faces*

**6** According to the economic theories, why do relationships end?

*profits and losses*

**7** What is the evolutionary explanation for passionate love?

*child-rearing advantage*

**8** What is the difference between marriage in collectivist cultures and marriage in individualistic cultures?

*arranged marriage*

# Physiological Psychology

**5 minutes**

## Test your knowledge

1. The outermost covering of the brain is called the _____ _____ .

2. The forebrain is divided into the two _____ _____ which mirror each other in structure.

3. In a split brain operation to treat epilepsy, the _____ _____ is cut.

4. One of the most important brain structures in motivation is the _____ .

5. There are two types of thirst, called hypovolemic and _____ .

6. Feeding seems to be controlled by the _____ and _____ areas of the hypothalamus.

7. According to the drive reduction theory, an animal will not learn unless it is given _____ .

8. An important brain structure in emotion is the amygdala, which is part of the _____ system.

9. The _____-_____ theory of emotion suggests that we experience arousal and behaviour which we then label as an emotion.

## Answers

1 cerebral cortex 2 cerebral hemispheres 3 corpus callosum 4 hypothalamus
5 osmotic 6 ventromedial, lateral 7 reinforcement 8 limbic 9 James-Lange

**If you got them all right, skip to page 21**

# Physiological Psychology

**30 minutes**

## Improve your knowledge

| Key points from AS | AS in a Week reference |
|---|---|
| Methods for investigating the brain | page 43 |
| Divisions of the nervous system | pages 42–45 |
| The ANS, fight/flight response and stress | pages 45–48 |
| Bodily rhythms, sleep and dreaming | pages 51–55 |
| The cognitive labelling theory of emotion | page 46 |

**1** The cerebral cortex is the outermost covering of the brain. It is a thin sheet of neurones about 3mm thick with a wrinkled appearance that comes from the fact that it is folded in on itself many times. Only a third of the cortex is visible on the surface of the brain. Many of the brain's functions are localised in the cerebral cortex. That is, specific cortical areas deal with specific tasks. In general, a distinction can be made between three major types of cortical area:

- Sensory areas deal with incoming sensory information.

- Association areas process information.

- Motor areas produce behavioural responses.

An example of a localised function in the cerebral cortex is vision. This is primarily dealt with by the visual cortex, situated at the rear of the brain. Studies by Hubel & Wiesel (1959) showed that different clusters of neurones in the visual cortex of cats respond to different types of stimuli detected by the retina. Damage to the visual cortex in humans can result in a form of blindness in which they lose the part of their visual field to which the damaged portion of the visual cortex corresponds.

Interestingly, some people with such impairment show a phenomenon called blindsight. Although they do not consciously detect objects placed in the impaired section of their visual field they can point to them with surprising accuracy, even though they continue to insist that they can see nothing. This may indicate that other areas of the brain (particularly the superior colliculus) also play a role in vision.

**2** The forebrain is divided into two cerebral hemispheres. These two areas largely mirror each other. The structures found in one hemisphere are also found in the other. Each hemisphere is responsible for the opposite side of the body. So, for example, the left visual hemisphere processes information from the right visual field and vice versa. Similarly, damage to the right motor cortex results in impaired movement on the left-hand side of the body.

However, some brain functions are concentrated in one hemisphere. That is, some functions are lateralised.

Language areas in the left hemisphere

| Name of area | Main function | Result of damage |
|---|---|---|
| Broca's area | Speech production | Non-fluent aphasia: difficulty producing speech whilst comprehension may be relatively unimpaired. |
| Wernicke's area | Speech comprehension | Fluent aphasia: speech is fluent although there is usually difficulty naming objects (anomia). Comprehension is more impaired than with non-fluent aphasia. |

**3** Not only are some functions lateralised in the brain, it is widely believed that the two cerebral hemispheres function in generally different ways.

Some processing features of the left and right hemispheres
(based on Zimbardo, 1988)

| Left hemisphere | Right hemisphere |
|---|---|
| Linear (or serial) processing | Holistic (or parallel) processing |
| Verbal processing | Non-verbal processing |
| Memory of words and numbers | Memory of shape and music |
| Recognition of words | Recognition of faces |

Much of the support for the idea that the two hemispheres have generally different functions comes from studies carried out by Sperry on 'split-brain patients'. There are people who, in order to control severe epilepsy, have had their corpus callosum (the connection between the two hemispheres) cut. Sperry and his colleagues studied a group of people who had undergone this operation and found that they appeared to develop two separate consciousnesses, operating independently of each other.

In one of Sperry's experiments, split-brain participants were presented with photographs of different types of people (e.g. an old man, a young girl, etc.). The photographs were cut in half down the middle and mismatched halves put together (e.g. old man on one half, young girl on the other). The photos were presented to the participants in such a way that the left side was only visible to the right hemisphere and the right half was only visible to the left hemisphere. If the participant was asked to describe the photo (a left hemisphere activity) then they would describe the right side of the photo (e.g. 'a young girl'). However, if asked to point with their left hand to the appropriate picture from a selection (a right hemisphere activity) they would indicate the picture which corresponded to the left side of the photo (an old man). Sperry concluded that the split brain produces two different consciousnesses and that the processing features of each hemisphere illustrated hemispheric differences that apply to all people.

Not all researchers accept Sperry's conclusions. Two major problems that occur when Sperry's findings are generalised to non-split-brain people are:

- Sperry's participants had a long-term abnormality in brain functioning (i.e. epilepsy) which may have altered the organisation of their brain functions.

- In people with an intact corpus callosum, the two hemispheres cooperate very closely and are in constant communication with each other.

These criticisms mean that the findings obtained by Sperry from split-brain patients may not apply to the clinically normal population.

**4** A variety of structures in the brain are associated with motivation. Many of the most important motivational structures are situated in the hypothalamus. By electrically stimulating different parts of the hypothalamus, psychologists can cause an animal to engage in a variety of behaviours, including eating and drinking.

**5** Mammals become thirsty for two reasons. Osmotic thirst occurs when the concentration of solutes in the body rises (e.g. after eating something very salty). Hypovolemic thirst occurs when a large amount of fluid is lost from the body and blood pressure drops as a result. Osmotic and hypovolemic thirst are controlled by different brain mechanisms.

The concentration of solutes in the blood is monitored by receptors in the third ventricle of the brain and in a structure called the OVLT (organum vasculosum laminae terminalis). If the concentration of solutes rises, these structures signal to the lateral preoptic area of the hypothalamus, which controls drinking. Hypovolemic thirst is monitored by parts of the endocrine system and by baroreceptors which measure the pressure of blood returning via large veins to the heart. If blood pressure drops too low, the hormone angiotensin II is released. This stimulates the subfornical organ in the brain which, in turn, stimulates the lateral preoptic area of the hypothalamus, resulting in drinking behaviour.

**6** Another example of a motivated behaviour is eating. Like drinking, eating is under the control of structures in the hypothalamus. Feeding seems to be controlled by the lateral hypothalamus (LH). If the LH of a rat is damaged, it develops aphagia: the rat (or other animal) refuses to eat or drink and, if it is not force-fed, it may starve or die of thirst. The LH appears to be stimulated by receptors in other parts of the body, including the stomach and duodenum.

Another important structure in the control of feeding is the ventromedial hypothalamus (VMH). Damage to the VMH results in hyperphagia – an animal with a damaged VMH will eat far more than usual and put on a great deal of weight. The VMH appears to be part of the brain's satiety system, which tells the animal when to stop eating. However, it is not the only important structure for this. Damaging the paraventricular nucleus (PVN) can also induce hyperphagia, although the pattern of altered behaviour is different.

Animals with VMH damage eat normal-sized meals but feed more frequently. Animals with PVN damage eat much larger meals than normal.

**7** The drive reduction theory is a theory of motivation and learning based on biological factors. It suggests that organisms are motivated to act in various ways by the activation of drives. For example, if an animal has a glucose deficit its hunger drive will be activated. High levels of drive are uncomfortable for the animal and it is therefore motivated to do something (in this case, seek food) to reduce its drive level. Any behaviour which results in the eating of food will reduce the drive level, returning the animal to a more comfortable state. This will act to reinforce the behaviour which led to the drive reduction, meaning it will produce the same behaviour next time its hunger drive is activated. Drive reduction theory is therefore a version of the theory of operant conditioning (see *AS in a Week*, page 59).

One problem with the drive reduction theory is that it suggests that learning will not occur unless drive is reduced through reinforcement. Experiments by Tolman and Honzik (1930), in which rats were given the opportunity to learn their way through a maze without reinforcement, suggest that drive reduction is not necessary for learning to occur.

**8** A number of different brain structures are linked with emotion. Two of the most important are the hypothalamus and the amygdala, which is part of the limbic system. The limbic system consists of a series of structures located underneath the cerebral cortex. Stimulation of different parts of the limbic system results in displays of various emotional behaviours.

The amygdala seems to play an important role in anxiety and fear responses and plays a central role in producing the startle response to sudden stimuli. The amygdala receives inputs from several sensory modalities including pain and has outputs to the pons, which controls startle behaviours such as freezing and flinching. Rats with a damaged amygdala still produce startle responses to, for example, a loud noise. However, it is difficult to condition them to respond to fear signals. This suggests that the amygdala is important in the learning of fear responses.

The amygdala is also important in recognising fear in others. In people with Urbach-Wiethe disease the amygdala and surrounding areas of the brain gradually die. Such people experience fear very weakly and have great difficulty identifying fearful expressions in other people.

Another brain area implicated in emotion is the ventromedial hypothalamus, which also plays a role in feeding (see above) and sexual behaviours. Stimulation of the VMH can increase the likelihood of an animal attacking an intruder. Neurones in the VMH respond to testosterone which may help to explain the apparently higher levels of aggression in males.

**9** According to the James-Lange theory of emotion, the emotional responses we feel are based on the way our nervous system reacts to stimuli. So, for example, if we are confronted by a threatening stimulus, our nervous system will react by increasing arousal and producing behaviour (e.g. running away). We then label the emotion depending on what we are doing (i.e. 'I am afraid because I am running away').

There are a number of problems with the James-Lange theory. For example, it predicts that if no arousal is felt by a person they will experience no emotions. Studies of people who have lost all bodily sensation following spinal injury suggest that emotion is not lost although it may be felt differently (Lowe and Carroll, 1985). Many psychologists agree that the cognitive labelling theory of emotion (see *AS in a Week*, page 46) gives a better account of how our emotions function.

# Physiological Psychology

25 minutes

## Use your knowledge

**1** Why do we generally not notice that the two cerebral hemispheres have different processing features?

**2** How could you test the idea that the lateral preoptic hypothalamus controls drinking behaviour?

**3** Is it justifiable to say that the ventromedial hypothalamus is a feeding centre?

**4** How can drive reduction theory explain why negative reinforcement occurs?

**5** A psychopath is a person who appears to have a diminished ability to respond to fear in others. This may be due to abnormal brain functioning. Which brain area would you expect to be dysfunctional and how would you test this idea?

**Hint**

*how do they communicate?*

*what methods are available for studying brain function?*

*is it involved in any other function?*

*refer to AS in a Week, page 60*

*you need to be able to see which brain areas are working*

# Classification and Psychopathology

5
minutes

## Test your knowledge

**1** The system used to classify mental disorders by the American Psychiatric Association is the _____ and _____ Manual of Mental Disorders, 4th edition.

**2** Diagnosis is _____ if different clinicians give the same diagnosis to one individual.

**3** The group of psychotic disorders characterised by major disturbances in thought, emotion and behaviour is referred to as _____ .

**4** According to the dopamine hypothesis, schizophrenia might be linked to an _____ of the neurotransmitter dopamine.

**5** There are two basic types of depressive disorder, referred to as _____ disorder and _____ disorder.

**6** Phobias and obsessive-compulsive disorder are both examples of _____ disorders.

**7** When an individual induces vomiting or uses laxatives following an eating binge, they are diagnosed with _____ .

**8** When an individual is 25 per cent below their optimum body weight and refuses to eat, they are diagnosed with _____ .

## Answers

1 Diagnostic, Statistical 2 reliable 3 schizophrenia 4 excess 5 unipolar, bipolar 6 anxiety 7 bulimia 8 anorexia

 **If you got them all right, skip to page 33**

# Classification and Psychopathology

**30 minutes**

## Improve your knowledge

| Key points from AS | AS in a Week reference |
|---|---|
| Applying the psychodynamic approach to mental disorders | page 38 |
| Definitions and approaches to mental disorders | pages 65–68 |
| Eating disorders (anorexia and bulimia) | pages 69–70 |
| Dissociative identity disorder (multiple personality) | page 68 |

**1** It is necessary to classify abnormal behaviour into different disorders in order to identify causes and treatments. One major classification system is the Diagnostic and Statistical Manual of Mental Disorders 4th Edition (DSM IV), published by the American Psychiatric Association (1994). The distinguishing feature of DSM IV is multi-axial classification, that is, the patient is assessed separately on five separate axes (see the table below). Only axes I and II refer to actual mental disorders, the other axes refer to other information which might be relevant to diagnosis (e.g. axis IV might consider the stress an individual was placed under after losing their job).

DSM IV – Multi-axial classification

| **Axis I** | Clinical disorders (e.g. schizophrenia) |
|---|---|
| **Axis II** | Personality disorders and mental retardation. |
| **Axis III** | Medical conditions relevant to the mental disorders |
| **Axis IV** | Environmental and psycho-social stressors |
| **Axis V** | Social, occupational and psychological functioning |

**2** Reliability refers to whether different clinicians would give one individual the same diagnosis. Beck (1961) asked four experienced psychiatrists to interview 153 patients and found they only agreed on 54 per cent of cases. Reliability has been improved in DSM IV by making the information in the diagnostic manual more specific and using a standardised interview procedure. A diagnostic category (e.g. schizophrenia) is said to be valid if all individuals with that diagnosis show the same symptoms and respond to the same treatments. If not, it could be argued that the diagnostic class is actually referring to different types of mental disorder. In the UK it has been found that schizophrenia is over-diagnosed in young black men, suggesting that classification systems such as DSM IV show a cultural bias. For example, classification systems assume that people of a non-Western origin suffer from the same disorders as Western people. According to this view, clinicians must take into account the cultural factors which distinguish people in minority groups from the dominant culture in which they live.

 Schizophrenia refers to a group of psychotic disorders characterised by major disturbances in thought, emotion and behaviour, where the patient usually withdraws from people and reality, often into a fantasy life of delusions and hallucinations. There are two types of schizophrenic symptoms, positive and negative (see the table below). Positive symptoms refer to the bizarre experiences and beliefs that the patient tells the clinician about and are diagnosed by their presence. Negative symptoms (or more accurately signs) refer to abnormalities in behaviour, diagnosed by their absence.

Positive and negative symptoms in schizophrenia

| **Positive Symptoms** | |
| --- | --- |
| Paranoid delusions | Patients believe people are trying to harm them. |
| Delusions of control | Patients experience their actions as being controlled by outside forces. |
| Thought broadcast | Patients experience their thoughts leaving their mind and entering the minds of others. |
| **Negative Symptoms** | |
| Anhedonia | Loss of in interest in sex, intimacy and friendship. |
| Avolition | Poor hygiene, lack of energy and no interest in work. |
| Affective flattening | Lack of facial and vocal expression. |

Family and twin studies indicate that schizophrenia has a heritable component. That is, people who are closely related to schizophrenics are more likely than the general population to develop the disorder. Gottesman et al (1987) found a concordance rate of 0.40 for MZ (identical) and 0.11 for DZ (non-identical) twins. However, although these results show that schizophrenia has some genetic component, it is not 100 per cent genetic and it is likely that it develops from an interaction between a genetic predisposition and some environmental trigger. Possible environmental risk factors include exposure to a virus and stress.

 One biochemical theory of schizophrenia, known as the dopamine hypothesis, proposed that schizophrenia is linked to an excess of the neurotransmitter dopamine. Drugs that reduce the action of dopamine (e.g. chlorpromazine) reduce schizophrenic symptoms, whereas drugs that increase the action of dopamine (e.g. amphetamine) can worsen schizophrenic symptoms. However, many studies have found no direct evidence of any excess dopamine, but instead suggest a higher concentration of post-synaptic dopamine receptors. It is still unclear whether any changes are a cause of schizophrenia or a result of years of drug treatment.

There is no evidence that psycho-social factors can 'cause' schizophrenia, except in individuals already at risk. Two such factors which have been investigated are social class and communication patterns. The highest rates of diagnosis for schizophrenia are made in inner city areas inhabited by the lowest social classes. One interpretation is that the stress of living in a low social class (poor housing, education and employment) may trigger schizophrenia. The alternative is that because the schizophrenic individual cannot hold down a job, the choice to live elsewhere is removed. Although there is more support for the latter suggestion, most studies are inconclusive. Social class appears to play a role, but the exact way in which stressors exert their influence remains unknown.

Research has shown that when patients return home following a period of hospitalisation, the likelihood of relapse is in part determined by family communication patterns, in particular the level of negative expressed emotion (EE). Patients were more likely to relapse when relatives were hostile and critical in their communications (high levels of negative EE) and patients whose relatives displayed understanding and insight were less likely to relapse (low levels of negative EE). These results have been replicated with patients in community care, suggesting that the crucial factor is the communication between patients and whoever they live with, rather than specifically with the family.

There are two types of major clinical depression, unipolar and bipolar. Unipolar disorder refers to depression and bipolar disorder to alternating episodes of depression and mania, sometimes referred to as manic depression.

Symptoms of unipolar and bipolar disorder

**Depressive symptoms**
Feelings of worthlessness and guilt
Loss of appetite and libido
Lack of energy and interest

**Manic symptoms**
Hyperactivity and overconfidence
Racing thoughts and rapid speech
Frenzied and incoherent activity

Family studies have indicated a heritable component in depression. Relatives of unipolar depressives are also more likely to develop unipolar depression. Relatives of individuals with bipolar disorder are more likely to develop unipolar but not bipolar disorder. Although family studies are open to criticism because they do not control environmental factors, twin studies have also revealed a genetic component in depression. Allen (1976) compared the concordance rate in MZ (identical) and DZ (non-identical) twins for both unipolar and bipolar disorder and found the following results.

|  | MZ twins | DZ twins |
|---|---|---|
| Unipolar disorder | 0.40 | 0.11 |
| Bipolar disorder | 0.72 | 0.14 |

These results show a genetic component in depression, although bipolar disorder has a stronger heritable component than unipolar disorder. However, depression can only be partly genetic and results from twin studies must also be treated with caution as they may not fully control environmental factors.

One biochemical theory of depression, known as the serotonin hypothesis, proposes that depression is linked to a lack of the neurotransmitter serotonin (5-HT). Drugs that increase the action of 5-HT (e.g. Prozac) reduce depressive symptoms, whereas drugs that reduce the action of 5-HT (e.g. Reserpine) can worsen depressive symptoms. This hypothesis has received direct support from metabolite studies showing that depressives have low levels of 5-HT waste product in urine, therefore indicating a low level of 5-HT in the brain. However, it is still unclear why drugs like Prozac affect 5-HT within hours of ingestion yet take around two weeks to reduce depressive symptoms.

According to the cognitive theory, depression can be explained in terms of biased information processing. Beck (1967) proposes that depressive individuals distort information to fit in with a negative view of the world, themselves and the future. Although a range of studies show that depressives are negative and pessimistic, they may not always distort information as Beck thought. According to the learning theory, depression is a state of learned helplessness. Seligman (1974) suggested that when individuals unsuccessfully try to control traumatic events, they learn that nothing they do will help and so give up – they literally learn to be helpless. This results in a passive attitude and a sense of not being in control of one's own life.

The cognitive-behavioural theory is a synthesis of the cognitive and learning approaches. Abramson *et al* (1978) modified the theory of learned helplessness to include attribution theory (explanations for behaviour). When we experience failure, we have to attribute this failure to some cause. The depressed person has a biased attributional style in which they always attribute the cause of failure to themselves. Seligman (1979) provided support in a study where students were given an attributional style questionnaire and found that depressives blame themselves more often than controls do. Where students had high grade expectations but their actual grades were low, non-depressed students attributed the failure to some external event, while depressed students tended to blame themselves.

Anxiety disorders refer to mental disorders characterised by feelings of fear and apprehension, such as phobic disorder and obsessive-compulsive disorder. A phobic disorder refers to a fear-mediated avoidance response which is out of proportion to the situation or object causing it. Phobias are classified into three types.

| | |
|---|---|
| **Specific phobias** | Avoidance of specific objects (e.g. spiders) and situations (e.g. closed spaces) |
| **Agoraphobia** | Fear of public places, linked to tension, panic attacks and dizziness |
| **Social phobia** | Persistent and irrational fear generally linked to the presence of other people |

Family studies suggest a genetic component to phobic disorder in 45 per cent of cases, although most had different types of phobias. However, there is direct evidence that phobias can be learnt by imitating family members, so family studies can only provide superficial evidence for genetic cause. A twin study by Torgersen (1983) found a concordance rate of 0.00 for DZ twins and 0.13 for MZ twins. Taking into account the evidence that phobias can be learnt, twin studies cannot be said to provide any more reliable evidence for a genetic component in phobias than family studies.

One neurological factor which may predispose individuals to develop a phobia is the responsiveness of the autonomic nervous system (ANS). The ANS controls automatic fear reactions (speeding up heart-rate, dilating pupils, etc.) and so 'jumpy' individuals with an ANS which is over-responsive to environmental stimuli could be at risk of developing phobias. Support for this idea comes from a psychometric questionnaire, the EPQ (Eysenck & Eysenck, 1975), one scale of which (N-scale) measures ANS arousability. A range of studies have shown that phobic individuals tend to score highly on the N-scale, suggesting they have an ANS which is very easily aroused. One serious drawback of this theory is that ANS responses might simply be effects, rather than a cause of a phobia.

According to learning theory, the acquisition of phobias can be explained through classical conditioning and the subsequent avoidance of phobic objects through operant conditioning. In situations causing fear (e.g. a car crash), some people associate the car with the fear and subsequently develop a fear of all cars. The avoidance of cars is rewarding and becomes a habit. Although learning theory provides a theoretical explanation of phobic disorder it has two problems. Firstly, it does not explain why some fears are more common than others (e.g. snakes, spiders, the dark, etc.). Second, the majority of people who have a phobia have not undergone a traumatic event. In response to the first criticism, evolutionary theorists have suggested that there was a survival advantage for our ancestors in avoiding snakes, spiders, etc., and so we are 'biologically prepared' to avoid such stimuli. Regarding the second criticism, there is some evidence that we do not need a traumatic event to learn a phobia – we can learn a phobia through imitation, so we may copy fear responses from parents and other role models. However, this still does not explain where phobias originated from.

According to the cognitive approach, people develop social phobia (an excessive fear of social situations and the presence of other people) because of a bias in the way they interpret social events. Stopa & Clark (2000) supported this approach by asking pps to interpret a series of social events ranging from ambiguous to negative. Results showed that pps with social phobias interpreted ambiguous social events more negatively and negative social events more catastrophically than healthy pps. This interpretative bias increases the anxiety associated with social situations and prompts individuals to avoid social situations, making them less likeable.

Obsessive-compulsive disorder (OCD) is a severe chronic psychiatric problem. Obsessions are recurrent, persistent ideas that are experienced as intrusive or senseless (e.g. concern with dirt). Compulsions are repetitive purposeful behaviours perceived as unnecessary, that are performed in response to an obsession (e.g. excessive washing of hands).

According to the biochemical theory, there is a certain amount of evidence that OCD is linked to a lack of serotonin (5-HT), as drugs that increase the effectiveness of 5-HT (e.g. Fluoxetine) have been extremely effective in treating OCD patients. However, metabolite studies have found that OCD patients have normal levels of 5-HT waste product in their urine and so the evidence for the role of 5-HT remains indirect. As a result, some researchers have suggested that the therapeutic value of Fluoxetine in treating OCD is simply a by-product in lifting depression, but this does not seem to be the case. Most anti-depressants have no effect on OCD patients and the effectiveness of Fluoxetine on OCD does not depend on whether patients are depressed or not.

According to learning theory, compulsions are strategies for reducing the anxiety brought on by the obsession. For example, a patient who ritually cleans is reducing their anxiety about being dirty all the time. Self-reports of anxiety by patients support this idea, but not all compulsive acts reduce anxiety to the same degree. So although this theory can explain the existence of compulsions, it cannot explain where obsessive thoughts come from. The cognitive theory may be able to provide a solution by suggesting that obsessive thoughts arise from a cognitive bias known as thought-action fusion. Shafran (1997) showed that when OCD patients have an unwanted thought (e.g. my hands are dirty), they believe it is more likely to happen in reality and become preoccupied with it. The patient then becomes trapped in a cycle of reducing the anxiety associated with these thoughts by compulsive behaviours.

**7** The two most commonly studied eating disorders are anorexia and bulimia. Anorexia nervosa is a condition where individuals have an intense preoccupation with body size and a distorted body image; even those who are emaciated believe they are fat. It is diagnosed when an individual has lost 25 per cent of body weight and refuses to eat. These individuals are obsessed with food and will engage in frantic exercise to shed imaginary fat. They fear a loss of control, and show a lack of inner resources and self-esteem, a fear of sexuality and a fear of being controlled by others. Onset is usually in late adolescence and approximately 95 per cent of cases are women. The disorder causes physical problems including a loss of menstruation, low blood pressure and insomnia.

**8** Individuals with bulimia nervosa are also concerned with body image, with a morbid fear of becoming fat. Such individuals feel intense anxiety after eating and induce vomiting or use laxatives to avoid weight loss, and then experience feelings of shame, guilt, depression and a lack of control. The disorder is more common in women, tends to develop in the early twenties and can also lead to physical problems including loss of body fluids, loss of menstruation and severe tooth decay caused by stomach acid from vomiting.

Twin studies have suggested that eating disorders may be in part genetic. Treasure & Holland (1989) compared the concordance rates for MZ (identical) and DZ (non-identical) twins and found the following results.

|  | MZ twins | DZ twins |
|---|---|---|
| Anorexia | 0.43 | 0.06 |
| Bulimia | 0.35 | 0.29 |

These results show that for both anorexia and bulimia the concordance rate is higher for MZ twins, suggesting some genetic component in eating disorders. However, it should be emphasised that these results show that eating disorders can be only partly genetic. In addition, results from twin studies should be treated with caution as they may not fully remove environmental factors.

Lask (1997) developed a neurological approach by scanning the brains of children with anorexia whilst they were asked to carry out tasks like judging their body size. He found that regions of the brain dealing with visual perception on the temporal and occipital lobes showed reduced blood flow, indicating some type of malfunction. This may explain why anorexic individuals may see themselves as overweight when they are emaciated. These physical changes in the brain do not mean it is inevitable that anorexia will develop but they may provide a diathesis (a predisposition) to developing anorexia, where environmental triggers are required. These environmental triggers may include a period of stress and socio-cultural factors such as living in a society which pressures women to be thin. Even when physical changes are found in the brains of patients with eating disorders, it is not inevitable that these changes were responsible for causing the eating disorder. It is possible that these physical changes were not the cause, but the result of the eating disorder.

According to the socio-cultural theory, anorexia and bulimia are caused by pressure on women in Western society to be thin. There is an ideal shape for women presented by models and film stars which has become more and more thin over the past 30 years. For example, Garner et al (1980) examined the vital statistics of Playboy centrefold models from 1959 to 1978 and found that in contrast to the average weight of ordinary women, the models weighed 17%

less than the average for their height. The social pressure to become and stay slim has increased as ordinary women have drifted further away from the cultural ideal. This theory predicts that eating disorders will increase in incidence for groups where a premium is placed on thinness, and evidence tends to support this prediction. Crisp (1976) surveyed 16- to 18-year-old London schoolgirls and found that dancers and fashion models were more likely to develop the disorder. In addition, anorexia is much more common in Western cultures than in other cultures. However, this theory cannot explain why the majority of women exposed to social pressure to be thin do not become anorexic, so societal pressure can only be one contributing factor.

The cognitive approach has focused on irrational thought processes, in particular, distorted body image. Slade & Russell (1973) asked 14 hospitalised anorexic patients to estimate their body size. Results showed that they overestimated their size by 25 to 55 per cent, compared to a control group who made roughly accurate estimates.

Although results seem to suggest that body image disturbance is causing anorexia, Crisp & Kalucy (1974) found that while anorexic patients overestimated their body size after eating a fattening meal, so did a group of normal patients. One possible reason for the discrepancy in the results may lie in age differences in body perception. Shortly after these results were published it was found that ordinary people tend to estimate their body size more accurately as they grow older. As it happened, the control group patients in Slade & Russell's study were significantly older than the anorexic patients, and this may explain why the group of anorexics overestimated their body size more than the control group.

# Classification and Psychopathology

25 minutes

## Use your knowledge

Hint

**1** Why is it necessary to classify mental disorders?

causes and treatment

**2** Why is it important that diagnosis of mental disorders is reliable?

treatment

**3** What is the difference between positive and negative symptoms in schizophrenia?

use table on page 24

**4** Can schizophrenia be caused by socio-psychological factors?

social class and expressed emotion

**5** What is the difference between unipolar and bipolar depression?

use the table on page 26

**6** Describe the evidence for the serotonin (5-HT) hypothesis of depression.

anti-depressant drugs

**7** Do evolutionary factors play a role in phobias?

why are we scared of snakes and spiders?

**8** What is the evidence of distorted body image being a factor in eating disorders?

do people without eating disorders have a distorted body image?

# Therapeutic Approaches

**5 minutes**

## Test your knowledge

**1** Somatic therapies are based on the _____ _____ of psychological disorders.

**2** SSRI antidepressants increase activity at synapses that use the neurotransmitter _____ .

**3** Neuroleptic medication is used in the treatment of _____ .

**4** ECT stands for _____ - _____ _____ .

**5** Token economies are a behavioural therapy based on the principles of _____ conditioning.

**6** Cognitive behavioural therapies attempt to alter a client's _____ _____ through altering their behaviour.

**7** In psychoanalysis, the therapist helps the client to resolve _____ _____ .

**8** One problem with evaluating the effectiveness of therapies is that it depends heavily on which _____ _____ are used.

**9** According to Carl Rogers, the therapeutic relationship must have three features: _____ _____ and _____ .

 **If you got them all right, skip to page 43**

# Therapeutic Approaches

**30 minutes**

## Improve your knowledge

| Key points from AS | AS in a Week reference |
|---|---|
| Definitions of abnormality | pages 65–66 |
| Models of abnormality | pages 66–68 |
| Applying the learning approach | page 61 |

**1** Somatic (biological) therapies are based on the medical model of abnormality. This model holds that psychological disorders are caused by physical malfunction of the brain. The therapies attempt to restore psychological functioning by altering the functioning of the brain. Common somatic therapies include drugs, electro-convulsive therapy (ECT) and psychosurgery.

**2** Drugs work by altering the balance of neurochemicals in the brain. This is usually achieved by altering chemical events at the synapses in order to increase or decrease the firing of certain neurones. Two common drug therapies are antidepressants and neuroleptics.

Antidepressants are used in the treatment of unipolar depression and can also be used in the treatment of eating disorders and obsessive compulsive disorders. The table below shows the characteristics of three common antidepressants.

Antidepressant drugs

| Drug | Neurotransmitters affected | How it works |
|---|---|---|
| MAO inhibitors | Increases the activity of serotonin, dopamine and noradrenaline synapses | Blocks the action of monoamine oxidase (MAO), which would normally break these substances down, allowing them to stay in the synaptic gap for longer. |
| Tricyclics | Increases activity in serotonin and dopamine synapses. | Prevents the neurotransmitters from being taken back into the presynaptic neurone, allowing them to stay in the synaptic gap for longer. |
| SSRIs | Increases activity in serotonin synapses. | Prevents the re-uptake of serotonin only. |

Antidepressants bring about an improvement in the symptoms of around 60 per cent of depressed patients. They may take up to three weeks to have a positive effect. MAO inhibitors and tricyclics may cause severe side effects (including toxicity and heart problems) in some cases. SSRIs are believed to have less severe side effects, although in some people they may cause akathisia, a condition linked to aggression and suicide.

 Neuroleptic drugs are used in the treatment of schizophrenia. They work by binding on to dopamine receptors but not stimulating them. This prevents the naturally occurring dopamine in the brain from stimulating the synapse. Therefore, the activity of dopamine synapses is reduced.

Neuroleptic drugs bring about a therapeutic improvement in around 60 per cent of schizophrenic patients. However, there are a number of drawbacks associated with their use. They tend only to treat the positive symptoms of schizophrenia and not the negative ones (see the chapter on Classification and Psychopathology). They may cause severe side effects, including a movement disorder similar to Parkinson's disease. This is because the brain systems controlling movement rely on dopamine. When dopamine activity is reduced by the drug, these systems are affected. Newer drugs called atypical antipsychotics are less likely to do this. However, the new drugs are expensive and have other side effects (e.g. reducing the number of white blood cells).

 Electro-convulsive therapy (ECT) consists of passing an electrical current through the brain. It was initially developed as a treatment for schizophrenia but was found to be ineffective. However, it appears to be effective in the treatment of depression. It is unknown exactly how ECT works. ECT is effective in alleviating depressive symptoms in 60 to 70 per cent of depressed patients. It works more quickly than antidepressant drugs and is therefore used when the patient is at a high risk of suicide. However, clinicians avoid using ECT for a number of reasons including:

- It may cause side effects such as memory loss.

- Its effects are temporary and patients usually need further treatment within one year.

- It is a forceful and frightening treatment which, historically, has been used in abusive ways, for example, for controlling and punishing patients.

Psychosurgery involves the destruction of brain tissue through surgical means.

Psychosurgical procedures

| Procedure | Used in the treatment of | What it involves |
|---|---|---|
| **Pre-frontal lobotomy** | Schizophrenia | Severing the frontal lobes of the cerebral cortex from the rest of the brain |
| **Com-misurotomy** | Severe epilepsy | Severing the central commisure (or corpus callosum), which connects the two cerebral hemispheres, 'splitting' the brain |
| **Cingulotomy** | Severe anxiety disorders | Severing the cingulum nerve connecting the cerebral cortex to the limbic system |

Psychosurgery is a highly controversial technique and there is a continued debate as to its effectiveness. For example, the pre-frontal lobotomy was a very popular procedure during the 1950s but is no longer carried out as it was found not to be effective. In general, psychosurgery is used as a 'last resort' treatment because:

- All surgery carries a certain degree of risk.

- The effects of psychosurgery are unpredictable and there may be no benefits.

- Psychosurgery is irreversible.

 Behavioural therapies are based on the behavioural model of abnormality, which suggests that psychological disorders are learned behaviours. Behavioural therapies are an attempt to get the patient to 'unlearn' maladaptive behaviours and learn adaptive ones. Two behavioural therapies are systematic desensitisation (based on classical conditioning) and token economy (based on operant conditioning).

Systematic desensitisation is used in the treatment of phobia (an anxiety disorder). It is based on the idea that anxiety is a learned response to the phobic stimulus (i.e. the thing the person has a phobia of). The aim of systematic desensitisation is to replace the anxiety response with a relaxation response. There are a number of stages to systematic desensitisation. First, the client is taught a relaxation technique, so that they can relax at will. Then they are gradually brought into contact with the phobic stimulus over a number of sessions. This graduated exposure might initially consist only of visualisation and eventually graduate to handling the phobic stimulus. During contact with the phobic stimulus the client continues to relax. Eventually they will have learned to replace their original anxiety response with a relaxation response.

Systematic desensitisation is very effective in the treatment of phobias. Up to 80 per cent of phobic clients experience some improvement. The treatment is most effective for simple phobias (where the phobia is of a specific object, e.g. spiders). Other sorts of phobia do not respond so well. For example, although between 50 and 80 per cent of agoraphobics (fear of going outside) may experience some improvement, this is often slight and there is a high probability of relapse.

Token economies are a behavioural therapy used to treat the effects of long-term institutionalisation. Patients who stay long-term in a hospital or other institutional context may lose their ability to perform basic self-care tasks for themselves. In order to avoid this, token economies use the principles of operant conditioning to encourage positive behaviours amongst patients.

In the first stage, a list of desirable behaviours is drawn up. This might include self-care activities such as dressing in clean clothes, or making the bed each morning. Each time a patient performs one of these behaviours they are given a token. The tokens may be exchanged for things like chocolate, cigarettes, days out or the opportunity to choose television programmes. The tokens act as positive reinforcers, increasing the likelihood that the patient will perform desired behaviours in future.

Token economies seem to be effective at promoting self-care behaviours within institutions. However, the benefits of token economies do not seem to last once the patient rejoins the community. There are a number of other issues associated with the use of token economies. These include:

- In order for tokens to be valued, access to basic goods like cigarettes and chocolate must be restricted. Some psychologists consider this to be unethical.

- It is unclear whether the improvements in token economies result from the reinforcement value of the tokens or for other reasons (e.g. better organisation of wards and more frequent positive interactions between staff and patients).

 Cognitive behavioural therapies (CBT) are based on the assumption that psychological disorders reflect maladaptive thinking strategies. CBT aims to alter the way the client thinks through altering their behaviour.

CBT has two main elements. In the cognitive part of the therapy, the therapist carefully questions the client in order to identify potentially harmful, irrational or self-defeating beliefs. Rather than challenging the beliefs directly, the therapist treats them as hypotheses about the world. In the behavioural part of the therapy, the client is set 'homework' in which these hypotheses are tested. If the client can demonstrate to themselves that some of the beliefs they hold about the world are untrue they may be motivated to change them.

CBT has been shown to be successful in treating a wide variety of psychological problems including depression and anxiety. It can also be used in conjunction with drug therapies to reduce the delusions experienced by schizophrenic patients. CBT-based therapies are popular in the NHS as they are short-term and have a clear structure and goals, which makes the outcome of the therapy easy to assess. However, one problem with measuring the effectiveness of CBT is that it is difficult to define exactly which beliefs are irrational. It is also the case that psychologically healthy individuals think irrationally at least some of the time.

 Psychoanalytical therapies are based on the psychodynamic model of abnormality which suggests that psychological disorders are caused by high levels of conflict in the unconscious mind. The original therapy developed by Freud is now referred to as classical psychoanalysis. A more recent development of the therapy is called brief psychodynamic therapy (BPT).

Classical psychoanalysis involves a number of techniques through which the therapist uncovers potential conflicts or repression in the client's unconscious mind. The table overleaf shows the most frequently used of these.

Techniques of classical psychoanalysis

| Technique | What it involves | How it works |
|-----------|-----------------|--------------|
| **Free association** | The client reports the free flow of images, thoughts and feelings as they enter, unforced, into their mind. | As long as the patient is not thinking too hard, the thoughts will reflect unconscious connections and themes. |
| **Word association** | The therapist reads out a list of words. The client responds to each one with a word of their own. | The client's responses reflect unconscious associations with the therapist's words. |
| **Dream analysis** | The client records the dreams they have and discusses them with the therapist. | The symbolism of the dreams reflect unconscious desires which are interpreted by the therapist. |
| **Projective tests** | The therapist shows the client a series of pictures or inkblots. | The client reports their impressions or tells a story about them. The client's interpretations are influenced by their unconscious motivations and associations. |

The aim of psychoanalysis is to bring about transference, where the client transfers repressed feeling onto the therapist. Once this happens, the therapist can identify them to the client and work them through, reducing the levels of unconscious conflict in the client's mind.

One of the major problems with classical psychoanalysis is that it may take years for the client's problems to be worked through and the therapy is thus both time-consuming and costly for the client. More recently, brief psychodynamic therapy (BPT) has been developed to address these problems. It uses many of the same techniques of classical psychoanalysis but has several distinctive features:

• The therapy is time limited to around six sessions.

• Symptoms are addressed directly, rather than underlying conflicts.

• Rapid improvement is expected.

• Transference is not encouraged.

**8** The question of the effectiveness of psychodynamic therapy was initially broached by Eysenck (1952). Eysenck compared clients receiving psychotherapy with clients on a waiting list and concluded that, whilst 66 per cent of clients receiving no treatment improved, only 44 per cent of those receiving psychotherapy did so. He concluded that the improvement rate for clients receiving psychodynamic therapy was no better than the spontaneous remission rate (i.e. the rate at which clients would get better on their own) and that psychoanalysis may actually delay recovery.

Since Eysenck's original paper, many other researchers have examined the effectiveness of therapies and questioned his conclusions. The results of Eysenck's study relied on him measuring improvement in a particular way. Studies that use other outcome criteria to assess improvement generally indicate that psychotherapy is more effective than no therapy. However, it is more appropriate for the treatment of some disorders (e.g. depression) than others (e.g. schizophrenia).

**9** Humanistic or person-centred therapies are based on the work of Carl Rogers. Rogers believed that psychodynamic and behavioural therapies were too directive (i.e. they centre around telling the client what to think or do). Humanistic therapies attempt to create conditions under which a client can 'self-heal' and become a more empowered and confident person.

Rogers suggested that the most important thing in therapy is the relationship between the client and the therapist. In humanistic therapies it is believed that the therapeutic relationship should have three key features:

* Warmth (or 'unconditional positive regard'). The therapist must have respect for the client and accept them completely as a person.

* Genuineness. The therapist should show themselves to be a 'real' person with thoughts and feelings of their own. This may involve the therapist telling the client about themselves, something that would be avoided in psychodynamic and behavioural therapies.

* Empathy. The therapist must empathise with the client and try to understand how they see the world. This empathy must be demonstrated to the client through active and attentive listening to what the client has to say.

The aim of humanistic therapy is not to cure the client. Rather, the aim is to create the conditions under which the client can explore their understanding of the world and solve their own problems.

Humanistic therapies are now widely used and have been applied in many contexts. The therapies are not restricted in their usefulness just to people with diagnosed psychological problems and have been applied in a number of settings including stress counselling for employees, marriage guidance, bereavement and so on.

Many people feel that they have benefited from humanistic counselling. However, it is more helpful for some problems than others. For example, a person with severe depression might benefit more immediately from drug or cognitive behavioural therapies. Similarly, some clients may be unwilling to 'open up' to the extent required by a humanistic approach and therefore may be more comfortable with a more directive, behavioural therapy.

# Therapeutic Approaches

**25 minutes**

## Use your knowledge

**Hint**

what causes depression?

costs and benefits of treatment

is it likely to actually cure the disorder?

they explain psychological disorders differently

what factors might affect choice of therapy?

which factors cause ethical problems in other therapies?

1. What is the major disadvantage of using drugs to treat depression?

2. Which ethical issues arise from the use of neuroleptic medication?

3. Why is the pre-frontal lobotomy no longer used in the treatment of schizophrenia?

4. How do behavioural therapies differ from cognitive behavioural therapies?

5. Why is classical psychoanalysis relatively rarely used compared to other forms of therapy?

6. Why are humanistic therapies sometimes called the most ethical form of treatment?

**5 minutes**

## Test your knowledge

1. Criminological psychology is the application of _____ principles to criminal behaviour.

2. Biological theories of crime explain criminal behaviour in terms of _____ and damage to the _____ .

3. Raine (1997) suggested that potential violent offenders can be identified using _____ _____ .

4. Eysenck's personality theory of crime proposes that people with high levels of extroversion and _____ are more likely to become criminals.

5. In offender profiling, an attempt is made to identify the characteristics of an offender from the _____ they leave at the crime scene.

6. British and American approaches to offender profiling differ in the extent to which they believe offenders can be assigned to rigid _____ .

7. According to Loftus, eye-witness testimony can be distorted if the witness is asked _____ _____ .

8. Hypnosis has been found to make witnesses less _____ but more _____ in their testimony.

9. If a jury deciding on the level of damages to be awarded in a case is prone to group polarisation, then their recommendations are likely to be _____ .

10. In cognitive restructuring interventions for criminal behaviour, an attempt is made to change the _____ that support criminal activity.

### Answers

1 psychological 2 genetics, brain 3 brain scans 4 neuroticism 5 evidence 6 types/categories 7 leading questions 8 accurate, confident 9 excessive 10 cognitions/thinking

 **If you got them all right, skip to page 53**

# Criminological Psychology

**30 minutes**

## Improve your knowledge

The effects of media on antisocial behaviour are covered in chapter 1, Social Psychology.

**1** A criminal is someone who transgresses the judicial laws of the society in which they live. Criminological psychology is the application of psychological knowledge to criminal behaviour. The aims of criminological psychology include:

- explaining why people commit criminal acts;

- helping the authorities to apprehend criminals, for example, through offender profiling;

- understanding the psychology of the courtroom;

- rehabilitating criminals so that they do not reoffend.

**2** Biological theories of criminal behaviour suggest that certain criminal acts are committed because the person is influenced by their biological characteristics. These might include:

- a genetic predisposition to crime;

- brain damage that makes certain criminal behaviours more likely.

The genetic approach to crime suggests that people may inherit certain genetic characteristics that make criminal behaviour more likely to develop. Researchers have attempted to identify genetic contributions to crime by comparing identical or monozygotic (MZ) and non-identical or dizygotic (DZ) twins. If criminality has a heritable component, then we would expect higher concordance rates for criminality in MZ twins.

Concordance rates for criminality in MZ and DZ twins (male only)

| Study | MZ concordance rate | DZ concordance rate |
|---|---|---|
| **Christiansen (1977)** | 35% | 13% |
| **Dalgaard & Kringlen (1976)** | 26% | 15% |

Although the slightly higher concordance rates for MZ twins suggest a genetic contribution to criminality, this is likely only to be slight. In Dalgaard & Kringlen's study, the difference was not statistically significant. Additionally, it is not clear exactly how genes might contribute to certain criminal tendencies. For example, there is unlikely to be a gene for burglary. It may well be the case that we cannot treat criminals as a single class of people and that genetic tendencies may exist for certain crimes and not others.

**3** Raine (1997) suggests that a pattern of brain damage affecting six areas of the cerebral cortex might be responsible for violent behaviour. The pattern of brain damage was identified using brain scans on prisoners convicted of violent assaults. A control group of non-violent offenders did not show the same pattern of damage. Raine suggests that those particular brain areas (presumably damaged during birth) are responsible for impulse control and that people in whom they are damaged are unable to control violent impulses.

Although Raine's findings are interesting, they do not account for all, or even most, examples of violent criminal behaviour. It is not yet known whether people with this particular type of brain damage inevitably become criminals. It is also the case, since there is no way of reversing this type of brain damage, that there is no obvious way to treat this sort of behaviour. Raine's suggestion that potential violent offenders should be identified using brain scans early in life is considered unethical by many commentators.

**4** Eysenck (1977) has suggested that certain personality types are predisposed to criminal behaviour. Eysenck's original theory proposed that there are two important underlying dimensions to personality. These are:

- Extroversion (E) – a measure of how much stimulation a person requires from their environment
- Neuroticism (N) – a measure of how stable a person is.

Eysenck believed that, to a great degree, a person's score on each of these scales was genetically determined. He suggested that people with high scores on measures of extroversion and neuroticism were most likely to become criminals since they require a high degree of excitement and stimulation and are more difficult to condition. They are therefore less likely to learn from their punishments and mistakes.

Although Eysenck's own studies have shown a relationship between personality scores and criminality, other researchers have questioned his conclusions. Blackburn (1993) concluded that the evidence does not support Eysenck's prediction that prison inmates should typically have high E scores. Hollin (1989), however, suggests that offender populations are characterised by higher than average N scores. Overall, Ainsworth (2000) concludes that, whilst there is no direct relationship between personality and criminality, it is likely that personality is one of a number of contributing factors which may result in criminal behaviour.

Offender profiling is an attempt to predict the characteristics of an offender from the evidence they leave at the scene of a crime. It is rarely employed and used almost exclusively in cases of serious, serial crime such as murder and rape.

In the US, the Federal Bureau of Investigation (FBI) has pioneered the use of offender profiling. The FBI's approach was originally based on extensive interviews with 36 sexually-orientated serial murderers and analysis of the crimes they had committed. On the basis of this evidence, researchers attempted to identify the typical personality and behaviour of such offenders. One distinction made by the FBI is between organised and disorganised offenders.

Organised and disorganised offender characteristics (Hazelwood, 1987)

| Offender type | Offence characteristics | Offender characteristics |
| --- | --- | --- |
| **Organised** | Well planned; few clues left; target is a stranger | Above average intelligence; socially and sexually competent; likely to be living with a partner |
| **Disorganised** | Spontaneous and poorly planned; little attempt to destroy evidence | Living alone, probably close to scene of crime; socially and sexually inadequate; mistreated as a child |

Other classification systems developed by the FBI include one in which rape attacks are assigned to one of four types. The behaviour of the rapist towards the victim and the apparent degree of planning involved allow the investigators to make an assessment of the motive for the attack and the likelihood that the rapist will attack again. These classification systems also allow investigators to assess the probability that different offences were carried out by the same person.

Although the FBI's profiling system is well known (especially since films like *The Silence of the Lambs*) and has helped to solve a number of serious crimes, it is not without its critics. Many researchers suggest that the sample on which it was based is too small to permit generalisation. It is also the case that the way the system is applied in practice is rather subjective. Different investigators can emphasise different aspects of the same crime and arrive at very different conclusions about the characteristics of the person who committed it.

In the UK, Canter (1994) has adopted a different approach to that of the FBI. Canter's approach is based on three assumptions:

- A given individual will become involved in a particular sort of crime and will carry out these crimes in a distinctive way.

- The way an individual commits a crime will mirror their behaviour in everyday life.

- A criminal's actions at the scene of the crime will reveal certain things about their background.

The main difference between Canter's and the FBI's approach is that Canter does not attempt to place offenders into rigid categories. Rather, his approach is based on the idea that the way an offender commits a crime will reflect their personality, experience and behaviour.

One aspect of Canter's work concerns relating the location of an offence with the offender's mental map of the area. People's mental maps of their locality are often distorted compared to the actual geography of the area. This is because mental maps are based on the person's experience of moving around rather than on an objective geographical view. Canter suggests that, when planning an offence, an offender will draw on their mental map of the area and, unwittingly, restrict their activities to certain locations. Canter has found that the majority of rapes he has studied took place less that two miles from the rapist's home. Davies & Dale (1995) have confirmed that, in three-quarters of cases, the rapist lives less than five miles from the location of the offence.

Canter's approach to crime location can be very valuable to police forces as it allows them to concentrate their investigation in a particular area. Once psychologically relevant aspects of the offence location (e.g. the presence of CCTV cameras, street-lighting, possible escape routes) have been taken into account, police can identify with a high probability the area in which an offender lives. They can also take steps to prevent crime by eliminating possible crime 'hotspots' where potential offenders may choose to operate.

Although some of the evidence regarding offender profiling is impressive it should be remembered that a profile rarely, if ever, directly results in the solving of a crime. At best, offender profiles can assist police investigations by allowing investigators to direct their resources more effectively. For example, investigations can be concentrated on particular locations or police attention diverted towards particular types of suspects (Ainsworth, 2000).

 Often, when a person is put on trial for a particular crime, the criminal proceedings will rely to a certain extent on eyewitness testimony (EWT). In order for the legal system to work effectively, we must be confident that EWT is accurate. Some researchers have suggested that EWT can be distorted by the way police and lawyers ask questions.

Loftus suggests that police and lawyers often ask witnesses leading questions which introduce information about the events that took place. This information can be unwittingly incorporated by the witnesses into their memories, resulting in unreliable testimony. Loftus & Zanni (1975) showed participants a film of an accident involving two cars. Their recall of the accident was assessed using questionnaires. Different groups of participants were asked slightly different questions. For example, the participants were asked to estimate the speed at which the cars were travelling. All were asked, 'How fast were the cars going when they...', but for different groups, the final word of the question was changed. This had an effect on the participants' estimates (see the table overleaf).

Results of Loftus & Zanni's (1975) experiment

| Final word | Mean estimate of speed (mph) |
|------------|------------------------------|
| Hit        | 34.0                         |
| Bumped     | 38.1                         |
| Collided   | 39.3                         |
| Smashed    | 40.8                         |

Loftus concluded that a word like 'smashed' suggests a more violent impact than 'bumped', leading participants to 'remember' the cars travelling at a higher speed. In a later experiment, participants who were asked the 'smashed' form of the question were far more likely than a control group to report having seen broken glass, even though there was none in the film.

Other researchers have questioned Loftus' conclusions. They point out that Loftus' participants and real witnesses are different in a number of ways including:

• Loftus' participants viewed films and not real events.

• Real witnesses may be in a state of high arousal.

• Loftus' participants may have been responding in the way they thought the researchers wanted.

Yuille & Cutshall (1987) interviewed witnesses of a real crime in which two people had been shot in broad daylight. They found that witnesses were able to supply a great deal of accurate information about what they had seen and were not susceptible to attempts to mislead them. It should probably be concluded that EWT (eye-witness testimony) can be distorted by leading questions, but not to the extent to which Loftus proposes.

Some police forces have used hypnosis to elicit EWT in the belief that it leads to more accurate recall. This is probably not the case. Putnam (1975) found that, under hypnosis, participants were less accurate than non-hypnotised participants in their recall of an accident. However, they were more confident in their answers. Since the apparent confidence of a witness has a great impact on the extent to which a jury believes them, it would be dangerous to allow such testimony to be used. Many judicial systems no longer allow hypnotic testimony to be used in court.

 A safe trial relies on the notion that juries are rational and objective in the way they examine and weigh up evidence to reach a verdict. Some psychological research suggests that this is unlikely to be the case. Social psychological studies of group decision-making have indicated that a number of different processes can operate within groups which may distort the decision that the group makes.

Group processes that may affect jury decisions

| Group process | What it involves | Possible outcome |
|---|---|---|
| Conformity | A person in the minority feels pressured to agree with the majority. | Sceptical jurors will not 'fight their corner' about the case if they are in the minority. |
| Leadership | The leader of a group has considerable influence over the behaviour of group members. | The jury foreperson will have undue influence over the verdict of the jury members. |
| Group polarisation | The view reached by a group tends to be more extreme than that reached by the members individually. | When asked to make a recommendation (e.g. about compensation) the jury will be excessively punitive or lenient. |

Although these processes have been well established in general research and research using mock juries, the extent to which they apply to real juries is not clear. The reason for this is that legal systems the world over have been extremely reluctant to allow psychologists access to juries to conduct research. Many legal systems even forbid jurors from discussing the cases on which they deliberate (Ainsworth, 2000). However, the processes identified above have proven extremely robust in other research settings and there is no compelling reason to believe that juries are completely exempt from them.

 Given that psychologists have spent considerable research effort trying to understand the causes of criminal behaviour, it may well be the case that they can play a role in preventing criminals from reoffending.

Most researchers agree that simply imprisoning offenders does not prevent them from committing further offences. Some attempts have been made to apply established psychological therapies in an attempt to reduce reoffending after release from prison. Two of these are outlined in the table below.

Two psychological interventions used with offenders.

| Therapy | What it involves | Outcomes |
|---|---|---|
| Token economy | Offenders in an institution are reinforced for desirable behaviours with tokens (see the chapter on Therapeutic approaches). | Although the management of offenders within the institution may become easier, there is little evidence that TEs reduce reoffending. |
| Cognitive restructuring | The beliefs which offenders have that sustain criminal behaviour (e.g. 'everybody does it') are targeted in an attempt to change them. | There is some evidence that CR is effective in preventing recidivism, at least for certain types of crime (e.g. shoplifting). More research is required. |

In the 1970s, the view arose that psychological interventions were wholly ineffective in altering criminal behaviour (Martinson, 1974). However, recent reviews of the evidence suggest that the 'nothing works' view is unduly pessimistic. Vennard & Hedderman (1998) propose that offender rehabilitation programmes are likely to be effective if they:

- target high-risk offenders;

- target factors such as drug dependency which contribute directly to criminal behaviour;

- match teaching methods to offender characteristics;

- challenge the attitudes and values which support criminal behaviour;

- are community based.

# Criminological Psychology

**25 minutes**

## Use your knowledge

**Hint**

**1** Why is it unlikely that one theory will ever explain criminal behaviour?

*is a criminal a certain type of person?*

**2** Why can personality alone not explain why a person becomes a criminal?

*a person does not exist in a vacuum*

**3** What are the potential disadvantages of using offender profiling to track down a criminal?

*how might it lead to errors?*

**4** Does Yuille & Cutshall's (1987) research invalidate Loftus' findings regarding eyewitness testimony?

*was it a typical crime?*

**5** Why, from a behaviourist point of view, is imprisonment on its own unlikely to result in a reduction in criminal behaviour upon release?

*think about conditioning and punishment*

**5 minutes**

## Test your knowledge

**1** The patient-practitioner relationship usually refers to the relationship between the _____ and _____ .

**2** One of the most important predictors of patient recovery is whether they adhere to medical _____ .

**3** One technique used to manage pain through learning how to control heart-rate and other ANS processes is _____ .

**4** Stress is said to occur when an individual perceives that _____ made on them exceed their ability to _____ with them.

**5** Physiological dependence on a drug is said to occur when an individual experiences symptoms of _____ and _____ .

**6** A significant predictor in health is the kind of _____ that people have.

**7** School-based programmes aim to promote healthy behaviour through _____ .

**8** Ill-health caused by bad work practices could be the result of a workplace _____ or an occupational _____ .

 **If you got them all right, skip to page 63**

# Health Psychology

**30 minutes**

## Improve your knowledge

| Key points from AS | AS in a Week reference |
|---|---|
| Stress and illness | pages 46–48 |

**1** The patient-practitioner relationship usually refers to the relationship between the doctor and patient. This is important for the study of health psychology because the success of treatment depends in part on this relationship in a number of ways. The exchange of information between doctor and patient will affect diagnosis and compliance with medical requests (e.g. to take medication). Beckman & Frankel (1984) recorded consultations between doctor and patient and found that in 69 per cent of cases the doctor interrupted the patient, patients spoke for an average of 18 seconds before being interrupted and in only 23 per cent of cases was the patient allowed to finish speaking. This 'controlling' technique used by the doctor prevents patients from discussing their concerns and leads to the loss of information important for diagnosis. Evans *et al* (1991) found that medical students who had been trained in communication skills were better at making a diagnosis because they were able extract more relevant information from patients. This research shows that accurate diagnosis does not just depend on physical symptoms but psychological factors. The use of specialised terms and jargon by the doctor may create a barrier between doctor and patient. WHO (1993) suggest that doctors should carefully monitor the amount of jargon they use, especially the use of frightening terms (such as 'cancer' or 'lump'), and give reasons behind diagnosis and management of the condition.

**2** One of the most important predictors of patient recovery is whether they adhere to the medical advice from their doctor. Ogden (1996) found that up to 50 per cent of patients with chronic illnesses such as diabetes and hypertension do not comply with their medication regimes and compliance is not related to the seriousness of the disorder. Ley (1989) developed a cognitive model of patient compliance (see table overleaf), where compliance is predicted on the basis of three factors: satisfaction with the consultation process; understanding of medical advice and recall of medical advice. With regard to patient satisfaction, Ley found that 28 per cent of GP patients and 41 per cent of hospital patients were dissatisfied with their treatment. Dissatisfaction came from different aspects of the consultation with the doctor including emotional (e.g. lack of understanding and support), behavioural (e.g. lack of explanation) and competence (e.g. problems over referral). Perhaps one reason why patients do not adhere to advice is that they are not satisfied with their treatment.

Predicting patient compliance (Ley, 1989)

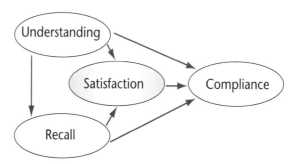

Regarding patients' understanding, Boyle (1970) asked patients to define several illnesses and found that only 85 per cent could correctly identify arthritis, 80 per cent bronchitis and 52 per cent palpitations. Roth (1979) found that 50 per cent of patients thought there was a good chance of recovering from lung cancer (although in fact it is fatal) and 30 per cent thought that hypertension could be cured when in fact it can only be managed through changes in lifestyle. Perhaps another reason for non-compliance is that patients do not have a good understanding of their condition and its treatment. Even if patients are satisfied with their treatment and have good understanding of their illness, if they cannot remember advice then compliance will be lower. Bain (1977) found that 37 per cent of patients could not remember the name of the drug they had been given and 23 per cent could not recall the frequency of the dose.

 There are two basic theories of pain, specificity theory and pattern theory. According to the specificity theory, we have special nerve cells for carrying pain messages from the skin to the brain. This model is oversimplified because it is now known that we have different types of nerve cells which respond to different types of pain. Pattern theories suggest there is no special neural system for pain – basically the same neurones react to ordinary sense like touch and pain. One example of a pattern theory is known as the gate control theory (Melzack & Wall, 1965). This theory suggests we have a 'gating mechanism'

which opens and closes in response to various factors. An injury will cause pain receptors to open the 'gate' sending pain messages to the brain. Rubbing an injured area or thinking about something else, will close the 'gate' and stop pain messages from travelling to the brain. This model highlights the need for psychological as well as physical factors in explaining pain. However, there is no direct support for the 'gating mechanism'.

It is possible to measure pain through physiological and behavioural measures and self-reports. Physiological measures include trying to measure muscle tension and brain activity in response to painful stimuli. Unfortunately, these measures do not accurately correspond to people's experience of pain and so lack reliability and validity.

Pain can be observed in behaviour such as limping and grimacing and some studies have trained spouses to note and observe such behaviour without reinforcing it. Whilst this method may have high ecological validity because it was carried out in the home, the coding of pain behaviour might not be so reliable. The self-report method is to ask people to report their perceptions of pain over a period of weeks or months in a diary. There are a number of advantages to this approach: it looks at pain from the point of view of those experiencing it and it charts how pain levels fluctuate over periods of time. However, self reports are subjective and cannot provide an accurate or objective measure of pain levels.

Psychological techniques for the management and control of pain include biofeedback and cognitive behavioural therapy. The idea behind cognitive behavioural therapy is that patients can reduce their subjective experience of pain through changing their interpretation and meaning of being in pain. In one strategy known as inoculation training, patients are taught to construct a mental immunity to the pain by thinking differently about the source of the pain experience. This technique has shown some success especially when combined with relaxation, although benefits depend upon the localisation and intensity of the pain. Biofeedback is a technique where patients can learn to control biological systems. For example, it is possible to control heart-rate through a monitor which produces a higher tone as heart-rate increases and a lower tone as heart-rate decreases. This technique has been successfully used in the treatment of migraine headaches and Reynaud's disease (constricted blood flow to fingers or toes). Although it is effective, it has been suggested that this technique works by decreasing arousal in the sympathetic nervous system and so is simply another form of relaxation therapy.

 Stress is a general term used when an individual feels the demands placed upon them exceed their perceived ability to deal with them. The transactional model of stress (Lazarus & Folkman, 1976) emphasises that the interpretation of stress is more important than the events which cause stress themselves. However, a number of sources of stress have been identified including control, predictability and change. A number of studies have shown that people experience more stress when they have little or no control over a situation (e.g. a traffic jam). In one study, pps were shown slides of violent deaths where one group of pps were told they could control exposure time and the other group had no control. The exposure time for both groups was actually the same, but the group who thought they were in control experienced less stress (Geer & Maisel, 1973). Events that are unpredictable (e.g. natural disasters) cause more stress. Katz & Wykes (1982) showed that pps who could predict a series of electric shocks experienced less stress than those who could not. If a stressor is predictable, it allows people time to prepare for it. Significant changes to a person's life (e.g. marriage, new job) can cause stress through disrupting normal routines. Evidence comes from the Social Readjustment Scale (Holmes & Rahe, 1976) which shows that significant life changes preceeded the onset of illness.

Stress can be measured in a number of ways. Stress involves a physiological response and so one method is to measure these physiological responses to stress. One technique is to measure changes in the ANS (autonomic nervous system). However, ANS arousal is produced by other emotions such as excitement and so does not tell us how an individual is feeling. Another technique is to measure the effects of stress. For example, rats develop stomach ulcers very quickly in response to stress. The problem with this approach is that the procedure causes suffering to the rats and results may not be generalisable to humans. The self-report method is to ask people to report their perceptions of stressors and experience of stress over a period of weeks or months in a diary. There are a number of advantages to this approach: it looks at stress from the point of view of those experiencing it and it charts how stress levels fluctuate over periods of time. However, self reports are subjective and cannot provide accurate or objective measures of stress levels.

Psychological approaches to the management of stress focus on changing the way people think and behave. Certain people with a personality type known as hardiness are resistant to stress and so one strategy to reduce stress is to train people in hardiness. For example, to see change as a challenge rather than a threat, to face problems and solve them rather than running away from them and to have some control over one's actions. The Hardiness Institute in California claims that by developing these hardy attitudes individuals will become more stress resistant. Another technique is stress inoculation, based on the idea that people can become stress resistant. Stage one is to consider alternative ways of coping with stress. Stage two is to learn skills for dealing with stressful situations (learning positive self-statements and rejecting negative self-statements). Stage three is to appraise performance. This approach can help people reduce stress by providing strategies to help them gain control and deal with the causes of stress, but has been criticised because the strategies do not deal with the actual causes of stress (e.g. overwork).

 Substance use refers to recreational drug use. Substance abuse occurs where the individual shows impaired functioning – for example, the drug user cannot maintain relationships or hold down a job. These are not legal definitions and can apply equally to legal drugs (e.g. alcohol) and illegal drugs (e.g. cocaine). Physiological dependence or addiction is said to occur when an individual experiences symptoms of withdrawal and tolerance. Tolerance is a physiological process whereby greater and greater amounts of the drug are required to produce the same effect. Withdrawal symptoms occur when the person stops taking the drug, and include anxiety, sweating and shaking. Some drugs such as ecstasy do not cause physiological dependence, but may cause psychological dependence because many of that person's activities are centred around the drug and characterised by a compulsion to take the drug because of its pleasant effects.

Drugs that affect an individual's mental state are referred to as psychoactive. They work by changing the way neurotransmitters operate at the synapse. Drugs that increase the action of a neurotransmitter are known as agonists and drugs that reduce it are known as antagonists. Cocaine is a dopamine agonist which works by blocking the re-uptake of dopamine (thus prolonging its effects) in the area of the brain which responds to pleasure. Cocaine is classified as a stimulant because of its psychological effects producing excitement, alertness, decreased fatigue and increased motor activity and is taken for its euphoric effects caused by directly stimulating the pleasure centre of the brain. Several hours after taking the drug, the users 'crash' and experience a depressed state as the excess dopamine is washed away faster than dopamine is synthesised. Prolonged cocaine use can cause psychosis where people experience delusions and hallucinations (note that schizophrenic symptoms of delusions and hallucinations are also linked to dopamine). For years, investigators could not explain the action of marijuana, however, recently it has been discovered that it is an anandamide agonist, stimulating canabinoid receptors in certain regions of the brain: hippocampus, basal ganglia and cerebellum. Marijuana has mostly sedative effects, promoting sociability and relaxation. In large doses it can have hallucinogenic effects, intensifying sensory experience, and causing time distortion and anxiety. Contrary to popular belief, marijuana is addictive, but less so than coffee! Tolerance quickly develops but withdrawal effects are relatively minor.

 The study of an individual's lifestyle is central to an understanding of health. For example, approximately 50 per cent of deaths in the West can be attributed to lifestyle. Two behaviours which can contribute to a healthy lifestyle are physical exercise and diet. Physical exercise has both physical and psychological benefits. Research has shown that the physical benefits include weight control and protection against heart disease, some kinds of cancer and stroke. Psychological benefits include reduced stress, depression and anxiety, and increased self-esteem. Research has shown that nutritional factors (e.g. foods containing carcinogens) in diet can account for 40 per cent of all cancer in men, and 60 per cent of all cancer in women in the USA. In the British diet, high levels of salt are linked to hypertension and heart disease and high levels of cholesterol to heart disease. Vitamins A, C and selenium are thought to play a role in preventing cancer.

Psychologists have investigated reasons why people continue to engage in unhealthy behaviours (e.g. smoking, lack of exercise) despite knowing about their potential threat. One reason might be that reluctance of people to accept that some aspect of their lifestyle requires changing. When we act in ways which we know are maladaptive (e.g. smoking cigarettes when we know they cause disease) we tend to defend ourselves. So when people are presented with health-related information, the *more relevant* the message, the *less likely* that person is to accept that message. Liberman & Chaiken (1992) provided support for this idea, using a fictitious report linking caffeine and breast disease. Women for whom the threat was most relevant (regular coffee drinkers) were less likely to believe the accuracy of the report than women who did not drink coffee. When a message contains a relevant health threat, this increases anxiety and the easiest way to reduce this anxiety is to disregard the information rather than to change lifestyle or behaviour. According to the health belief model (Becker & Maiman, 1975) the likelihood of an individual engaging in a particular health behaviour depends upon: threat of disease, severity of illness, benefits of treatment and individual variables (e.g. age, class, personality). The problem with this model is that it assumes that decision-making is rational. A stronger predictor of health behaviour is whether people think they are capable of changing their behaviour.

 The promotion of healthy behaviour through education and advertising is an example of primary prevention. This can take the form of posters in the dentist's waiting room (remember to clean your teeth), TV adverts (AIDS, heart disease, heroin, etc.) and school-based programmes. There have been several school-based programmes attempting to discourage young people from starting smoking. One such programme is based on the theory of reasoned action. Many children and adolescents believe that smoking is more prevalent than it actually is, establishing a norm that smoking is acceptable. Some programmes try to correct these normative expectations by providing factual information about true prevalence. The idea is that by establishing conservative norms (smoking is not acceptable), children and adolescents will be less likely to start smoking. Research into AIDS prevention has focused on changing sexual practices. One such programme, based on the health belief model, suggested the following principles would form the basis of an effective programme:

- emphasise the risk of certain behaviours;

- make clear the vulnerability of people who engage in such behaviours;

- demonstrate how changes in behaviour can reduce risk;

- persuade people that changes involve no inconvenience and loss of satisfaction.

Health and safety is usually taken to refer to accidents that occur in the workplace and work-related ill-health, which can be both mental and physical. Occupational disease (ill-health caused through bad work practices) is linked to factors in the physical environment such as noise, heat, length of time a person works, and time of day or night. For example, machinery operating above 90 decibels may impair hearing and so workers must only operate such machinery for short periods followed by a rest in a quiet area. The psychological effects of occupational disease can be harder to establish, but chronic work overload and role conflict can lead to stress, anxiety and depression. Young men have been traditionally more likely to have accidents in the workplace and a variety of factors have been suggested as causes: personality traits, inexperience with machinery and bravado over ignoring safety precautions. Hansen (1989) carried out a survey on 362 workers in the chemical industry and found that people who were more likely to have accidents were socially maladjusted and neurotic. Cognitive ability, age and length of service were all unrelated. It has been estimated that personality factors can only account for 10 per cent of workplace accidents and the three personality types most likely to have accidents are extroverts, neurotics and type A personalities (impatient and hostile). Organisations have a moral and legal responsibility to provide employees with assurance over safety at work and if not, employees can sue for compensation. It is not always easy to demonstrate that disease is related to the workplace. Lung cancer could be caused through exposure to radiation at work or a lifetime of smoking. In the case of computer operators suffering from repetitive strain injury, there is a much clearer relationship between ill-health and occupation and organisations now have to provide computer operators with enough space to change position and move.

# Health Psychology

## Use your knowledge

**1** Why is the patient-practitioner relationship important?

**2** Is it possible to predict whether patients will adhere to medical advice?

**3** Evaluate one method for measuring pain.

**4** What sort of things do individuals perceive as stressful?

**5** What are the psychological effects of cocaine?

**6** Use the health belief model to explain why people might not change to more healthy behaviours.

**7** How can healthy behaviours be promoted using the health belief model?

**8** What kinds of people are at risk from workplace accidents?

**5 minutes**

## Test your knowledge

**1** Statistical analysis is used to decide whether patterns in data are likely to have been caused by _____ .

**2** A _____ is a prediction about what the results of research are likely to be.

**3** If the probability of a set of results occurring by chance is above 0.05 then researchers will usually accept the _____ hypothesis.

**4** Interval level data have been collected on a scale of measurement which has _____ _____ .

**5** In order to check the significance of a set of results, a calculated statistical value must be compared with a _____ _____ .

**6** _____ methods concentrate on the meaning of a set of data.

**7** In _____ _____ large amounts of qualitative data are organised into themes in order to interpret them.

**8** Discourse analysis is often used to analyse naturally occurring _____ .

**9** Some researchers object to qualitative analysis on the grounds that it requires too much _____ interpretation.

**Answers**

✔ **If you got them all right, skip to page 71**

# Statistics and Research Methods

**30 minutes**

## Improve your knowledge

| Key points from AS | AS in a Week reference |
|---|---|
| Experimental methods | pages 73–75 |
| Correlational analysis | pages 75–76 |
| Observational studies | page 76 |
| Interviews and questionnaires | pages 77–78 |

**1** Psychologists use inferential statistics to analyse numerical data. The aim of inferential statistics is to allow researchers to judge whether a set of results was likely to be caused by chance. If this is unlikely, the results are said to be significant. If the results of an investigation are significant then it is usually assumed that they were caused by the effect being investigated.

For example, imagine that a researcher was investigating whether men or women are more likely to drive through an amber light at a road junction. The following data might be obtained:

|  | Female | Male |
|---|---|---|
| Drove through amber | 12 | 37 |
| Stopped at amber | 42 | 5 |

Statistical analysis would reveal that the likelihood of these results occurring by chance is less than 1 in 100. It might be concluded that the results indicate a gender difference in driving behaviour that requires further explanation.

**2** When inferential statistics are used, an alternative hypothesis is being tested. A hypothesis is a prediction about what the results of an investigation will be. Hypotheses should be clear and unambiguous. For the above investigation the alternative hypothesis might be:

*More men than women will drive through an amber light.*

This is a one-tailed hypothesis because it predicts not only an effect (a difference) but also a direction for that effect (i.e. more men than women).

Hypotheses should only be one-tailed when there is clear justification for suggesting the direction of the effect. A two-tailed hypothesis predicts an effect but no direction. An equivalent two-tailed hypothesis to the one above would be:

*There will be a difference between the numbers of men and women who drive through an amber light.*

Accompanying the alternative hypothesis is a null hypothesis which states that what is predicted will not actually happen. The usual way of stating this is to say that any effect observed will be due to chance. Returning to the above example, the null hypothesis would be:

*Any observed difference in the numbers of men and women driving through amber lights will be due to chance.*

**3** The inferential statistics used to analyse the data calculate the probability that the null hypothesis is correct. This information can be used to decide whether to accept the alternative hypothesis. The alternative hypothesis is accepted if the result is significant. It is up to the researcher to decide how unlikely the result must be before the alternative hypothesis is accepted – that is, decide what the minimum level of probability is. Usually researchers will not accept that a result is significant unless there is less than a 1 in 20 probability that the result was caused by chance. This is usually written '$p<0.05$'. If a researcher wants to be really confident that their results were not caused by chance, they may only accept the alternative hypothesis at $p<0.01$ (or 1 in 100).

**4** There are a number of different statistical tests which have different applications. It is very important to use the appropriate test for the data generated by the research. If the wrong test is used, the result will be invalid. In order to select the appropriate test it is necessary to answer three questions:

- Does the hypothesis predict a difference, correlation or association?
- Are the data nominal, ordinal or interval level?
- Are the data related or unrelated?

The table below explains what is meant by these terms.

| Question | Explanation | | |
|---|---|---|---|
| **What does the hypothesis predict?** | The hypothesis will indicate whether it is expected that two data sets will be different, that two variables will correlate or that two variables will be linked in some way (i.e. associated). | | |
| **What type of data?** | Nominal | The data consist of frequencies divided up into categories (e.g. number of male and female). | |
| | Ordinal | The data can be arranged in rank order. | |
| | Interval | The data were obtained using a scale of measurement with equal units (e.g. centimetres or seconds). | |
| **Related or unrelated?** | This depends on which research design was used (see AS in a Week). Repeated measures design yields related data. Any other design yields unrelated data. | | |

Once you have the answer to these three questions it is possible to select the appropriate statistical test using the information below.

When to use different statistical tests

| What does the hypothesis predict? | What type of data? | Related or unrelated? | Test to use |
|---|---|---|---|
| **Association** | Nominal | related | binomial sign test |
| | | unrelated | chi-squared test |
| **Correlation** | ordinal | related | Spearman rho |
| | interval | related | Pearson s product-moment |
| **Difference** | ordinal | related | Wilcoxon signed ranks |
| | | unrelated | Mann-Whitney U |
| | interval | related | related t-test |
| | | unrelated | unrelated t-test |

Once the statistical calculations have been made using the appropriate test, the result of these is called the observed value of the statistical test. For example, if the chi square test has been used, the result is called the observed value of chi square. The observed value is used to decide whether the result is significant. In order to make this decision, it is necessary to work out the degrees of freedom (or 'df') for the test. This is a number based on the sample size that gives an indication of how much variability is expected in the data. It is also necessary to decide the minimum acceptable probability ('p value'). This information is used to obtain a critical value from the table of critical values for the test used. The table below shows part of a table of critical values for the chi square test.

Critical values of chi square

| Prob. | (two tailed) | 0.10 | 0.05 | 0.01 |
|---|---|---|---|---|
| | (one tailed) | 0.05 | 0.025 | 0.005 |
| | df | | | |
| | 1 | 2.71 | 3.84 | 6.64 |
| | 2 | 4.60 | 5.99 | 7.82 |
| | 3 | 6.25 | 7.82 | 9.84 |

If we have carried out a chi square test and obtained an observed value of 5.43. With df = 2 and minimum acceptable probability $p < 0.05$ (one tailed) then the critical value will be 4.60. This is compared with the observed value of chi square. Since the observed value is higher than the critical value, the result is accepted as significant, since there is less than a 1 in 20 probability that it occurred by chance. Whether the observed value has to be higher or lower than the critical value to be significant depends on the test being used. This information is given in the table below.

Does the observed value need to be higher or lower than the critical value?

| Test | Higher or lower? |
|---|---|
| Chi square | Higher |
| Binomial sign test | Lower |
| Wilcoxon signed ranks | Lower |
| Mann-Whitney U | Lower |
| t-test (related) | Higher |
| t-test (unrelated) | Higher |
| Spearman s rho | Higher |
| Pearson s product-moment | Higher |

# Statistics and Research Methods

 The statistical analysis of data is a quantitative research methodology as it concerns itself with gathering data in the form of number. An alternative approach is to adopt a qualitative research approach. Rather than gathering data in the form of numbers, qualitative approaches focus on the meaning of data gathered from a variety of sources. These might include unstructured interview data, field notes and a variety of secondary sources such as newspaper articles.

 Qualitative analysis can take a number of different forms. Two important qualitative methods are thematic analysis and discourse analysis.

In thematic analysis, the material to be analysed is grouped together into the distinct themes it represents. The themes may emerge directly from the analysis of the data. For example, in analysing interview material gathered from students studying psychology, their opinions on the subject might fall roughly into two groups, one that sees the subject as interesting and relevant, another that sees the subject as difficult and boring. Researchers may prefer to decide which themes are likely to occur before analysing the data, in which case the themes and categories are likely to have been derived from theory. What is important to remember in thematic analysis is that the participants' reasons for saying what they say are extremely important. Qualitative methodologies typically concentrate on the perspective of the participants and how they understand things, rather than simply counting the numbers of particular behaviours they produce.

 Discourse analysis is a term which is applied to a wide variety of techniques. These tend to concentrate on analysis of naturally occurring speech and written materials although other materials (such as scientific papers or books) may be analysed. Different researchers tend to focus on different aspects of discourse: some may be interested in the way people use different linguistic strategies to manipulate a conversation whereas others might be more interested in the way metaphors are employed to make certain points. Still others tend to relate discourse analyses to wider debates within society concerning gender, culture and sexuality.

Qualitative methodologies tend to be favoured by critical researchers in psychology and related fields. Critical thinkers have applied discourse analysis to psychology itself and this research has been very important in highlighting the issues of racism and sexism within psychological research. Researchers from more scientific perspectives in psychology may object to qualitative methodologies on the grounds that they require too much subjective judgement on the part of the researcher. However, qualitative researchers may equally point out that the 'objectivity' of qualitative research is largely an illusion, since it is the researcher who decides which behaviours are important to study and how to measure them.

# Statistics and Research Methods

**25 minutes**

## Use your knowledge

Hint

*use the tables on page 67*

**1** A researcher wished to establish whether organised information was more effectively recalled than disorganised information. She used two word lists. On one of them the words were organised into categories (e.g. foods, furniture, etc.). The other list contained the same words but arranged in random order. Two groups of participants were used, one for each version of the list. They were given one minute to study the list. The list was then taken away and they were asked to write down as many words as they could remember. The researcher was interested in which group would recall more words.

(a) Write a suitable one-tailed hypothesis for this experiment.
(b) How could the researcher have randomised the order of the second word list?
(c) Which statistical test could be used to analyse the results?

**2** A researcher analysed a set of results using the chi square statistical test. The observed value of chi square was 3.27, with df = 3 and a one-tailed hypothesis.

*you will need a critical value for chi square*

(a) What is a suitable minimum acceptable level of significance?
(b) Were the results significant at this level?

**3** Does a researcher have to adopt either a quantitative or a qualitative approach when conducting research?

*can both be used?*

# Perspectives, Debates and Ethics

5 minutes

## Test your knowledge

**1** For psychology to be considered as a science, its data must be _____ and its methods must be _____ .

**2** According to the _____ perspective, psychological phenomena are learnt through experience of the environment. From the _____ perspective psychological processes are inborn and do not depend on experience.

**3** The scientific principle that it is possible to understand complex phenomena by breaking them down into their constituent parts is referred to as _____ .

**4** Research that takes American and European standards as the norm is said to show a _____ bias.

**5** Research that takes male standards as the norm and compares females to this norm is referred to as _____ biased.

**6** The British Psychology Society publishes an ethical _____ of _____ for research using human participants.

**7** Where there may be direct consequences for the lives of individuals, research is referred to as _____ sensitive.

**8** Animals have been used in research because it is possible to carry out procedures which would be considered _____ if carried out on humans.

## Answers

1 observable, objective  2 nurture, nature  3 reductionism  4 culture
5 gender  6 code, conduct  7 socially  8 unethical

 **If you got them all right, skip to page 82**

# Perspectives, Debates and Ethics

**30 minutes**

## Improve your knowledge

This section refers to the synoptic element required in A2 level psychology. This requires knowledge of the core approaches studied in AS level psychology as well as issues which cover the breadth of the specification – debates and ethics.

**1** In AS psychology you will have covered the following core approaches: cognitive, social, physiological, developmental and individual differences (psychodynamic and learning). The table overleaf summarises the major features of each approach. There are various philosophical debates in psychology over the following issues:

- Free will versus determinism  Can we choose to act as we do (free will) or is behaviour caused by influences beyond our control (determinism)?

- Reductionism  Reductionism refers to the scientific principle that it is possible to understand complex things (such as human behaviour) by breaking them down into their constituent parts (such as activity in the nervous system).

- Nature versus nurture  This debate is concerned with whether human characteristics (such as IQ) are the product of our genes or our experience and environment.

- Psychology as a science  For psychology to be a science it must only use certain methods and its data must be observable and measurable. Is this always the case?

**2** Core approaches to psychology

| Approach | Area of study | Methods |
|---|---|---|
| **Cognitive** | The influence of mental processes on behaviour | Experiments<br>Case studies of brain damaged patients |
| **Social** | The influence of social and situational pressure on behaviour | Experiments<br>Field studies<br>Discourse analysis |
| **Physiological** | The influence of the nervous system, endocrine system and genetics on behaviour | Experiments<br>Brain imaging techniques |
| **Developmental** | How cognition and behaviour changes during childhood and later life | Observations<br>Longitudinal studies |
| **Psychodynamic** | The influence of the unconscious and early experience on behaviour | Case studies<br>Analysis of symbolism |
| **Learning** | The influence of environmental factors on behaviour | Experiments<br>Animal studies |

As can be seen in the table below, the majority of the core psychological approaches are deterministic, reductionist and scientific.

The position of the core approaches on the four debates

| Approach | Deterministic | Reductionist | Nature or Nurture | Scientific |
|---|---|---|---|---|
| Cognitive | | ✔ | | ✔ |
| Physiological | ✔ | ✔ | Nature | ✔ |
| Psychodynamic | ✔ | ✘ | | ✘ |
| Learning | ✔ | ✔ | Nurture | ✔ |

* Where spaces in the table have been left blank, they have nothing to offer that debate. The social and developmental approaches have been deliberately left out of this table because there are some elements that are deterministic, reductionist and scientific and other elements that are not.

# Perspectives, Debates and Ethics

Determinism versus free will

The common-sense view is that we have the ability to choose our own course of action. Within physical and political limits we have free will and because of this view we hold people to be responsible for their actions – a very important point in the law. Scientific psychology holds a very different view – that all behaviour has a cause and can therefore be determined. If behaviour can be determined then it can be predicted. For B.F. Skinner (a learning theorist), free will is an illusion and all behaviour can be explained through the processes of operant conditioning. Our behaviour is determined by the pursuit of things which have been reinforcing in the past and consists of responses which have previously been reinforced. One criticism of this approach comes from Heather (1976) who says it is a mistake to think that because behaviour appears to be highly predictable, no choice was involved. We may only be choosing to act in predicable ways to fit in with society.

**3** Another feature of scientific psychology is reductionism. The general principle is that complex wholes are explained in terms of the units that make them up. In psychology this would mean explanations in terms of brain functioning, then chemistry and eventually physics. This kind of approach can be seen in a quote by Crick (1994) who says:

> You, your joys and your sorrows, your memories and your sense of personality and free will, are in fact no more than the behaviour of a vast assembly of nerve cells and their associated molecules.

One problem with this approach is that the meaning of psychological phenomena is lost when they are reduced to their constituent parts. For example, when we reduce personality traits to genetics we lose the meaning of personality. One solution offered by Rose (1976) is that psychology, biology, chemistry and so on, can provide different ways of explaining psychological phenomena, but one explanation cannot be used to replace another.

The nature-nurture debate applies to many areas of psychology such as IQ, personality and perception. Taking IQ as an example, from a nature perspective, behavioural geneticists believe that IQ is strongly influenced by genetic factors. From a nurture perspective, educationalists who have been working on enrichment programmes have seen how stimulating environments can improve the IQ of deprived children. Family, twin and adoptee studies seem to show superficial support for genetic factors but do not entirely remove the influence of environmental factors and so must be interpreted with caution. A recent study by Chorney *et al* (1998) using DNA coding found one gene (IGF2R) which is found in 28 per cent of high IQ children but only 13 per cent of average IQ children. The whole nature-nurture argument may stem from ignorance over how genes and the environment interact. They do not compete, as the nature-nurture debate suggests, but environmental factors determine which genes can express themselves in behaviour. Most researchers take an interactionist perspective, that genes and the environment combine to produce IQ, and debate the relative influence of genes and the environment.

In order to determine whether psychology is a science, it is first necessary to consider carefully what science actually is. Definitions of science usually suggest that data must be observable and the method must be controlled observation or experimentation. Most psychological approaches have observable data and use a scientific method but not all. In the cognitive approach, we cannot observe memory and attention directly, but these processes are inferred from participants' performance in experimental tasks. In the psychodynamic approach, we cannot directly observe defence mechanisms and the unconscious directly, but these processes are inferred from analysis of behaviour. Scientific methods must be replicable and controlled, involving the objective measurement of data. The cognitive approach can be said to use scientific methods through the use of lab experiments. However, psychodynamic methods are not usually considered as scientific because they do not involve objective measurement and are difficult to replicate. As a result, the cognitive approach is considered as scientific, because it uses the scientific method even though data is not observable. The psychodynamic approach is not considered as scientific because data is not observable and methods are not scientific.

**4** Critical theorists have argued that psychological theory and research is not objective and value-free but shows culture bias. Psychological theory is profoundly Eurocentric, steeped in the cultural values that are part of American and European life. Psychologists justify their biases (consider the race and IQ debate) in the name of science. Eurocentric standards in these theories are seen as 'normal', so cultures that do not share these norms are viewed as less well developed. The radical view is that science does not give us absolute truths but is a social construction that serves the interests of the dominant groups in America and Europe. Research can also be considered as Eurocentric in its choice of participants and methods. It is well known that much American psychology is based on studies using readily available white undergraduate students who can be invited, induced or expected to act as research pps. This group cannot be thought of as widely representative of other Americans, let alone other cultures, but is this issue a problem? Pps of other types rarely appear in the research literature, yet many studies generalise their findings to a North American and European population. In fact, it is a Eurocentric view that science should be favoured as the main route to knowledge and this itself is a form of bias. Other examples of culture bias in psychology can be found where research and theories developed in the West are universally generalised without question.

**5** Psychology before the 1970s was riddled with gender biases. Early male psychologists such as Stanley Hall claimed that women should not be allowed into higher education because education increases the blood flow to the brain and away from the uterus. With the rise of the feminist movement in the 1970s, feminist psychologists began to challenge limiting and demeaning views of women. The classic paper written in 1971 by feminist psychologist Naomi Weisttein was a scathing attack on psychology's theories about women. Psychology, she said, portrays women as inconsistent, emotionally unstable and intuitive rather than intelligent. In short, the list adds up to a typical minority group stereotype of inferiority. She pointed out that these kinds of psychological theories were used to keep women out of education and professional occupations, to confine women to the kitchen, the bedroom and the nursery, inferior to men in all aspects. Research which has shown that women have lower self-esteem and confidence than men is also gender-biased. This kind of research takes male standards as the norm and compares females to this norm. Another interpretation of these findings would be that women have normal levels of self-esteem and men are egotistical, or that women have normal levels of confidence and men overestimate their abilities. Other examples of gender bias in psychology can be found where research only uses male participants and generalises results to women without question.

The British Psychological Society (1993) published a set of guidelines designed to protect the rights of human participants. The most important of these are shown in the table below.

Ethical guidelines for research with human participants

| Informed consent | Pps should not be studied unless they give informed consent, which involves informing pps of the aim of the study and all procedures involved. |
| --- | --- |
| Deception | Pps should not be deceived over the nature of a study or any procedures involved in a study. |
| Debriefing | Following the study, researchers must be prepared to explain and discuss procedures and results with the pps. |
| Withdrawal | Pps should be made aware that they have the right to withdraw from a study at any point. |
| Confidentiality | Results should remain confidential and pps identities should not be revealed. In a case study, pps should be referred to by their initials (e.g. the case of H.M.). |

There are many examples of research which does not adhere to these principles. Researchers have claimed that in some cases it is necessary to deceive pps, since knowledge of the aims of such research would invalidate the results. In Milgram's study of obedience, if pps had been told that the shocks were not real then the study would not have made sense. Researchers justify deception by the importance of results and by debriefing pps afterwards. If pps have been deceived then it means they have not given informed consent. Once again, the argument goes that in certain studies, if pps were fully informed about aims and procedures then they either wouldn't take part or the study would lack realism, making results meaningless. Epstein & Lasagna (1969) discovered that only a third of pps volunteering for an experiment actually understood what was involved. Some pps who have given consent may later realise that they wish to withdraw and they should not be prevented from doing so even if they have received payment. In Milgram's study it appeared to the pps as if they could not withdraw from the study by the use of verbal 'prods' such as 'the experiment demands that you continue'. This may have been necessary to create pressure on the pps to obey – however, pps have the right to withdraw at any time. It might seem pertinent to ask what is the point of the guidelines if they keep being broken? This raises an important point that these guidelines are not 'rules' but guides to help researchers decide what is ethical and what is not.

**7** Where research has direct consequences for the pps or the group of people who the research is aimed at, it is referred to as socially sensitive. Although it could be argued that all psychological research is socially sensitive, there is no doubt that some research has more of a direct effect on people's lives. Examples of such research include Bowlby's 'maternal deprivation' hypothesis and the genetic basis of individual differences. In the 1950s, Bowlby claimed that children separated from their mothers even for short periods of time would suffer long-term consequences: social and intellectual retardation, delinquency and adult psychiatric problems. This had a direct effect on women's lives until perhaps the 1980s, despite research to the contrary. Women felt that to be a 'good' mother they had to stay at home and look after their children, denying them career opportunities. Those who were obliged to work had to live with the guilt of being a 'bad' mother. In the area of behavioural genetics, researchers have been trying to identify genetic influences in a range of individual differences such as IQ, personality and homosexuality. IQ testing has a controversial history. In the 1960s it was found that black Americans scored less than white Americans. On the basis of these tests, they were excluded from jobs and education, despite the fact that the IQ tests used had not been standardised for black Americans and were biased in the testing procedure. There are no BPS guidelines for the ethics of socially sensitive research, but Sieber & Stanley (1988) have identified ethical issues of special importance when dealing with socially sensitive research (see the table overleaf).

Ethical issues of special importance when dealing with socially sensitive research

| Privacy | Some research (e.g. behavioural genetics) may lead to an invasion of privacy (e.g. compulsory testing). |
|---|---|
| Sound and valid methodology | Some of the controversies that arise from socially sensitive research (e.g. race and IQ) arise from poorly designed studies. |
| Ownership of data | There is a worry that data could be used (e.g. by insurance companies) for reasons other than those for which they were originally intended. |
| Confidentiality | Confidentiality becomes of paramount importance when dealing with socially sensitive issues (e.g. drug use, AIDS research). |
| Risk / benefit ratio | Must be assessed very carefully — as benefits and risks may be harder to assess — and steps taken to minimise potential risks. |

**8** There are various arguments for and against the use of animals in psychological research. Scientific arguments for psychological research with animals rest on the idea that because humans and animals are evolutionarily related, it is possible to understand human behaviour through animal behaviour. It is possible to carry out procedures on animals that are not permitted on humans (see the chapter on Physiological Psychology). Animals make convenient pps. There is less emotional involvement (giving more objective results). Scientific arguments against the use of animals in psychological research argue that it is wrong to extrapolate findings from animals to humans because we are qualitatively different. Researchers are not always objective (because of anthropomorphism). We cannot learn about the complex aspects of humans which make us unique (e.g. language and culture) through animals. Ethical arguments against the use of animals argue that to discriminate and exploit another species is no better than racism or sexism. It is wrong to cause pain and suffering to animals. There have been attempts to add some scientific weight to this argument – it is assumed that those animals with a similar nervous system and behaviour to humans can feel pain as we do and so should not be subjected to painful procedures.

One way of resolving this debate is through weighing up the costs and benefits of animal research. Bateson (1986) proposed a model considering the certainty of human benefit, animal suffering and the quality of the research. So accordingly, if research is of a high quality, results are of definite benefit to humans and cause little animal suffering, then research is not unethical. Another alternative is to consider alternatives such as computer modelling and making full use of human case studies of deprivation and injury. There are two views as to how we should go about protecting animals in psychological research. Moral absolutism is the extreme view which believes that animal experiments should be completely banned. Moral relativism is a view adopted by the BPS that after weighing up various arguments, some research is permissible and some is not. The BPS (1999) issued guidelines for experiments on animals.

Ethical guidelines for research with animal participants

| Legislation | Researchers must familiarise themselves with laws regarding welfare, including which species are threatened. |
|---|---|
| Choice of species | Researchers require knowledge of species natural history and whether the animal has been born and bred in captivity. |
| Number of animals | Researchers should use the smallest number of animals possible through pilot studies, good experimental design and use of statistics. |
| Procedures | Any procedures which cause suffering require a Home Office licence. This requires licence holders to minimise pain, suffering and distress. |
| Housing and animal care | Responsibilities extend to conditions under which the animals are kept when not being studied, including freedom of movement. |

# Perspectives, Debates and Ethics

**25 minutes**

## Use your knowledge

**Hint**

assumptions and methods

the computer analogy

methods

see the table on page 80

consider the pros and cons

scientific, not ethical

Bateson's decision cube

1 Outline the main features of the cognitive approach.

2 How is the cognitive approach reductionist?

3 Is the cognitive approach scientific?

4 What special issues should be taken into account with socially sensitive research?

5 Should human participants be deceived in psychological research?

6 What are the scientific arguments against using animals in psychological research?

7 How can the debate for and against the use of animals be resolved?

# Exam Practice Questions

**90 minutes**

**1** Social psychology

Discuss two social-psychological theories of anti-social behaviour.  **[20]**

**2** Physiological psychology

Discuss whether brain function is lateralised (located in one hemisphere).

  **[20]**

**3** Classification and psychopathology

Discuss the possible contributions of social-psychological factors to the development of schizophrenia.  **[20]**

**4** Therapeutic approaches

(a) Describe any one therapy derived from the behavioural approach
  to mental disorders.  **[10]**
(b) Evaluate the therapy described in part (a).  **[10]**

**5** Criminological psychology

Discuss whether eyewitness memory can be considered as reliable evidence.

  **[20]**

**6** Health psychology

Discuss two psychological methods of health promotion.  **[20]**

Statistics and research methods

An experiment was carried out to compare the long-term effectiveness of antidepressant medication versus cognitive therapy. Eighty hospitalised patients diagnosed as suffering from clinical depression were randomly assigned to one of two therapy groups (either antidepressant medication or cognitive therapy). The therapy was considered successful if patients were discharged from hospital after one year. The following results were found:

|  | Antidepressant Medication | Cognitive Therapy |
| --- | --- | --- |
| Hospitalised | 18 | 5 |
| Non-hospitalised | 22 | 35 |

(a) What is the independent variable? **[1]**
(b) Write a two-tailed hypothesis for the above study. **[2]**
(c) What level of data is used in the above study? **[1]**
(d) Which therapy is the most effective? **[3]**
(e) Choose and justify a statistical test to analyse the data. **[3]**
**[10]**

 Perspectives, debates and ethics

Discuss the use of two ethical principles in research using human participants.
**[20]**

# Use your Knowledge
# Answers

## Social Psychology

**1** There are many lab experiments (e.g. Bandura) that support the social-learning approach but these do not address a number of issues. Firstly, these studies show that aggressive behaviour will be imitated in the short-term, but do not show whether aggressive behaviour will be repeated in the long-term. Second, these studies may lack ecological validity and so it is not clear whether the results are generalisable to everyday situations.

**2** Research has showed some links between environmental stressors and aggression, but often studies are inconclusive. We may become more aggressive as temperature increases, but when it becomes too hot we are more interested in escaping. Noise only seems to make us more aggressive when we cannot control it and crowding only seems to increase self-reported aggression in men not women.

**3** According to the empathy-altruism hypothesis, seeing someone else in distress arouses a feeling of empathy which motivates us to help. So we are helping for selfless reasons, because we care about the victim. According to the negative state relief model, seeing another in distress makes us feel bad and so our motivation is actually to remove our own negative feeling. Thus , although we may help another, our motivation is purely selfish – for our own benefit.

**4** There is a lot of research that says it does. Children watching TV programmes like *Sesame Street* are more likely to cooperate and help others afterwards. The evidence seems to indicate that when young children watch standard TV programmes where the main characters show concern and consideration for others, they will imitate these behaviours.

**5** According to the matching hypothesis we should be attracted to those with a similar level of attractiveness to ourselves. However, newer research has used computer-generated features to discover what we find attractive and what we do not. Studies seem to show that the most attractive face is the most average one – this is when a computer is asked to take the features from many different faces and produce the face with the most average features.

**6** The economic theories (social exchange and equity theory) would predict that when we get out less than we put into a relationship, or when favours are not repaid, we are likely to end that relationship. However, it seems that they do not take account of investment, that is, how much we have already put into a relationship.

**7** Evolutionary theorists have proposed that the most effective child-rearing strategy for humans is a male-female bond. For this bond to remain long-term, the couple must trust and have deep affection for one another. A brain chemistry has evolved to produce these feelings of trust and the label we give to these feelings is passionate love.

**8** In collectivist cultures, marriage is seen as a union between two families, whereas for individualistic cultures, marriage is based on love between two people. Consequently, marriages that have been arranged by the families are more common in collectivist cultures and represent responsibility to family and community values rather than the needs of individuals.

## Physiological Psychology

**1** In most people, the two cerebral hemispheres are connected by a large bundle of neurones called the corpus callosum. This allows the hemispheres to communicate very effectively. People only become aware of the processing features of the two hemispheres when their corpus callosum is damaged.

**2** A standard way of examining the role of different brain areas is to electrically stimulate them with small implanted electrodes. If the lateral preoptic hypothalamus of a rat was stimulated we might expect it to drink if water was available.

**3** No. The VMH plays a role in a number of different functions including feeding, sexual behaviour and aggression.

**4** Negative reinforcement occurs when an animal escapes from an aversive situation. The behaviour that allowed it to escape is strengthened. In drive reduction theory this is said to be because the aversive stimulation activates an escape drive. This drive is reduced if the animal gets away from the aversive stimulus and therefore, since drive reduction has occurred, the behaviour is reinforced.

**5** The amygdala seems to be the relevant brain area. We could test this idea using a functional MRI (see AS in a Week, page 43). We might expect to see heightened activity in a person's amygdala when they were shown pictures of people with fearful expressions. This could be compared with the brain response of psychopaths, whom we might expect to show much less amygdala activity when viewing fearful expressions. A similar experiment to this was carried out by Blair *et al* (1999), which confirmed the role of the amygdala in the processing of sad expressions in clinically normal people. However, it has not yet been confirmed that psychopaths respond abnormally in this respect.

## Classification and Psychopathology

**1** It is necessary to classify mental disorders so that they can be treated effectively. If different mental disorders have different causes then they will require different therapies. For example, a treatment for schizophrenia (e.g. the dopamine antagonist chlorpromazine) will have no therapeutic value with depression, which has different causes and therefore requires different treatments (e.g. 5-HT agonists).

**2** Reliability of diagnosis means that different clinicians (e.g. psychiatrists, psychologists, etc.) would give one individual the same diagnosis. This is important so that an individual will get the correct treatment for their disorder. For example, if an individual is diagnosed as depressed and subsequently treated with a 5-HT agonist when they are in fact schizophrenic, they will show no improvement, because they have been given the wrong treatment.

**3** Positive symptoms (e.g. hallucinations and delusions) are behavioural excesses, that is, they are found in schizophrenic patients but not found in clinically normal people. Negative symptoms (e.g. avolition and anhedonia) refer to behavioural deficits, that is, behaviour found in clinically normal people but absent in schizophrenic patients.

**4** Research seems to show that schizophrenia cannot be caused by socio-psychological factors alone. However, these factors may play a role in people already at risk. People in lower socio-economic groups are more likely to develop schizophrenia and hospitalised schizophrenics who return home to a hostile and critical environment (high levels of negative EE) are also more likely to be re-hospitalised.

**5** Individuals with unipolar depression experience symptoms of depression only (e.g. lack of energy and interest). Individuals with bipolar depression experience alternating symptoms of mania (e.g. frenzied and incoherent activity) and depression. They respond differently to treatments and also bipolar disorder seems to have a stronger genetic component.

**6** Anti-depressant drugs are 5-HT agonists, which work by increasing the effectiveness of 5-HT. Drugs that induce depression are 5-HT antagonists, which work by decreasing the effectiveness of 5-HT. It is not clear why anti-depressant drugs take two weeks to relieve symptoms of depression even though they affect 5-HT within a few hours.

**7** Certain phobias (snakes, spiders, the dark, heights, etc.) are more common than others and research has shown that monkeys will quickly imitate fear reactions to snakes but not flowers. Evolutionary theorists have proposed that there was a survival advantage in avoiding these objects for our ancestors and so we are biologically prepared to learn these fears more easily than others.

**8** Research has shown that people with eating disorders have a distorted body image: they think they are overweight when they are not. Initially it seemed as though the cause for eating disorders had been found. However, subsequent research has shown that ordinary people are no better at judging their body size than people with eating disorders. In conclusion, a distorted body image is not specific to eating disorders.

## Therapeutic Approaches

**1** The major problem is that the drugs may not tackle the root causes of depression. Although it is clear that drugs may benefit the patient by reducing the symptoms of depression, these may return once the drugs are discontinued. Many psychologists now believe that the ideal treatment consists of drugs to alleviate the symptoms in conjunction with some other form of therapy to address the reasons why the patient became depressed in the first place.

**2** Although neuroleptic medication can bring about benefits to schizophrenic patients, the side effects may be so bad that the person ends up no better off. If the patient is receiving minimal benefit from medication and it is causing severe side effects there seems to be little point in insisting they continue to take it.

**3** The chief effect of a pre-frontal lobotomy is to make the patient more docile. It has been argued that the operation has no therapeutic benefit beyond making the person more controllable. This is not actually curing the disorder. Additionally, the advent of effective antipsychotic medication meant there was a more viable treatment option for schizophrenic patients.

**4** The focus of behavioural therapies is the behaviour itself. This is because the behavioural approach assumes that the disorder consists of nothing more than its symptoms, which are learned behaviours. Cognitive behavioural therapies, on the other hand, suggest that the root of the problem is maladaptive thinking. The point of changing the behaviour is that it may alter the maladaptive cognitions.

**5** Classical psychoanalysis can take several sessions a week for a number of years. This is both time-consuming and costly. Compared to other therapies, classical psychoanalysis does not have clearly measurable goals and outcomes. The advent of shorter, more symptom-focused therapies has taken away some of the 'market share' that psychoanalysis once had.

**6** Ethical problems in therapies often arise from the fact that the client or patient is being told what to do or otherwise manipulated by an expert of some sort. Because humanistic therapies are non-directive, these types of problems are unlikely to occur.

## Criminological Psychology

**1** Much misunderstanding arises from the naïve belief that there is a certain type of person who is a criminal and that only 'criminal types' commit criminal acts. Most people will break the law at some point in their life. Similarly, people who would once have been considered criminals (e.g. homosexual men) no longer are. The fact that criminality is so widespread, varied and historically specific means that we must search for different explanations for different criminal behaviours.

**2** Personality can, at best, account for a predisposition to certain types of criminal acts. However, whether or not a person actually breaks the law will depend on both the experiences they have had and the opportunities presented to them.

**3** The actual usefulness of offender profiling has yet to be proven and there is always a possibility that the profiler will get things wrong. Problems may occur if the police investigation is based too much on the profile as this may lead to more useful lines of inquiry being ignored.

**4** Just as Loftus' research situation is not typical of eyewitnesses' experiences, neither is the situation investigated by Yuille & Cutshall, which involved a dramatic and violent incident played out in ideal witness conditions. For this reason we cannot use the study to totally refute Loftus' ideas, although it does indicate that witnesses can be very reliable.

**5** Imprisonment, looked at from a behaviourist point of view, is a punishment. A punishment is something that suppresses a behaviour (i.e. makes it less likely to occur). However, it does not teach the person anything new. In order to avoid reoffending it would be necessary to teach the person an alternative way of behaviour which did not involve crime.

## Health Psychology

**1** Research has shown that accurate diagnosis depends upon the doctor obtaining accurate information from the client. Successful treatment depends upon accurate diagnosis and so a good relationship between the doctor and patient is vital to the patient's well-being.

**2** According to Ley's (1989) model, patient compliance can be predicted on the basis of their understanding, recall and satisfaction. Patients who do not comply with medical advice tend to be dissatisfied with their doctor, do not have a good understanding of their illness and often forget what their doctor has told them.

**3** The self-report method is where people report their perceptions of pain over a period of weeks or months in a diary. These may have ecological validity, because they are carried out by the patient in real-life circumstances, but may not be reliable because our perception of pain is subjective. Comparing self-reports from one person to another is not reliable because people will have different tolerances to pain and difference ways of describing them.

**4** Research has shown that people experience events as more stressful when they have little or no control over the outcome of an event. When people can predict unpleasant or stressful events, then they tend to be perceived as less stressful, perhaps because we can put coping mechanisms in place. Significant changes in people's lives, even those normally considered as pleasant (e.g. holiday, marriage) can cause stress, perhaps simply through a change in routine.

**5** Initially, cocaine has a psychological effect as a stimulant, preventing drowsiness and promoting awareness and euphoria. Several hours after ingestion the user will experience a 'crash' typified by depression and lethargy. With regular use, tolerance quickly builds up and the user requires more and more cocaine to produce the same effect. Withdrawal symptoms include a constant craving for the drug and a feeling that one cannot cope without it. Persistent use can lead to 'cocaine psychosis', a psychiatric condition typified by hallucinations and delusions.

**6** According to the health belief model, people might engage in unhealthy behaviours (e.g. smoking) for a number of reasons. Firstly, they may not be aware of risks (e.g. threat of disease, severity of illness). Second, they may not be aware of the benefits of changing to healthy behaviours. Finally, individual variables will also have an effect (e.g. poor diet is associated with low socio-economic status families). This model assumes that people make decisions about whether to engage in healthy behaviour or not, which may not be the case.

**7** One AIDS prevention programme suggested the following advice based on the health belief model. First, emphasise the risks of engaging in unprotected sex and that AIDS is not only limited to high risk groups such as intravenous drug users and homosexual men. Second, demonstrate how changes in behaviour (i.e. using a condom) can reduce the risk of AIDS. Finally, persuade people that these changes involve no inconvenience or loss of satisfaction.

**8** It has been suggested that young men are more likely to have accidents because of inexperience and bravado over ignoring safety precautions, but personality factors have also been implicated. Research has identified that type A personalities, extroverts and neurotics are more likely to have workplace accidents, but these can only account for 10 per cent of cases.

## Statistics and Research Methods

**1** (a) 'Participants will recall more words from the organised list than from the disorganised list.' This is a one-tailed hypothesis as it predicts which group will recall more.

(b) By writing each of the words on a separate piece of paper and pulling them from a hat.

(c) The hypothesis predicts a difference, the data are at least ordinal level and they are unrelated since an independent measures design was used. Therefore the Mann-Whitney U test is appropriate.

**2** (a) p<0.05, since this is the usually accepted minimum.

(b) The critical value (df = 3, p<0.05, one-tailed) is 6.25. Since this is greater than the observed value (3.27), the researcher's results were not significant.

**3** Although some adherents of each approach discourage the use of the other there is no reason why a researcher should not use both. For example, in the classic studies by Stanley Milgram and Solomon Asch, quantitative data were given additional context and meaning through the addition of qualitative data derived from interviews with the participants after the research had taken place.

## Perspectives, Debates and Ethics

**1** The cognitive approach to psychology investigates the way in which we process information. Parallels are drawn between the way in which computers and humans process information in order to gain insights into human information processing. Cognitive processes cannot be directly observed themselves (e.g. we cannot actually see memory) but can be inferred from the behaviour of pps in experiments and brain-damaged patients.

**2** According to the cognitive approach, humans process information like computers and so the cognitive approach can be said to reduce psychological phenomena to the machinery inside people's heads. As a result, we end up with very individualistic explanations, locating psychological phenomena in terms of information processing.

**3** The cognitive approach uses strictly controlled lab experiments producing objective data to test falsifiable hypotheses and so seems to be scientific. It must be remembered, however, that cognitive processes (e.g. memory) cannot be directly observed and so results are interpreted in terms of information-processing. Therefore, cognitive explanations are analogies rather than concrete phenomena.

**4** Socially sensitive research may have a direct consequence on the person(s) being studied and so it is especially important that the results of such research will not infringe their privacy. Some people have suggested that research like the human genome project is socially sensitive in that it will lead to compulsory testing (which is an invasion of privacy) for predisposition to disease. Insurance companies may then discriminate against such individuals.

**5** Some research could not take place if pps were not deceived, as knowledge of the aim would change their behaviour. So we must ask what is more important, the rights of participants or the interests of psychological research. Some psychologists believe that deceiving pps is acceptable as long as they are not harmed in any way and are fully debriefed afterwards. However, this does run the risk of upsetting pps who will not take part in any psychological research in the future.

**6** It has been argued that we cannot learn anything about the unique qualities which make us human, such as language, culture and society, through the study of non-human animals. It has also been noted that researchers are not always objective when using animals and are prone to describing animals' emotional and cognitive states in human terms.

**7** One way of resolving the debate over whether animals should be used is to consider Bateson's decision cube: 1) certainty of human benefit, 2) certainty of animal suffering and 3) quality of research design. If animal suffering is low and human benefit is high then research should proceed. If animal suffering is high and human benefit is also certain the result would come down to the quality of research. If results would be vague and ambiguous then research should not take place.

# Exam Practice Answers

Exam questions in A2 level psychology require extended writing or essays. The following answers aim to provide guidance on how to answer these questions. Remember that in a real A2 level exam you will lose marks if you only list points.

**1** Remember you must cover two social-psychological theories. Because you are asked to 'discuss', you need to provide evaluation for these theories in the form of commentary such as criticism, support and limitations.

- According to the frustration-aggression hypothesis, aggression can occur when our pursuit of a goal is blocked.
- There is experimental support for this idea, but it is important to distinguish between frustration and deprivation.
- According to the social learning theory, aggression is learnt through modelling (imitating) others.
- Bandura's studies provide experimental support, but effects may not be long-term.

**2** Research suggests that some brain functions are lateralised (located in one hemisphere) whereas others are bilateral (found in both hemispheres). Because you are asked to 'discuss', you need to provide evaluation for research in the form of commentary such as criticism, support and limitations.

- Motor control and processing of sensory information (such as hearing and touch) is bilateral (mirrored in both hemispheres).
- The left hemisphere looks after the right side of the body and vice versa.
- Split-brain studies suggest that some functions (e.g. language) are lateralised (located in one hemisphere).
- Findings from split-brain patients may not be generalisable to the normal population.

**3** Possible social-psychological factors include social class and family communication patterns. Because you are asked to 'discuss', you need to provide evaluation for such factors in the form of commentary such as criticism, support and limitations.

- The highest rates of schizophrenia are found in the lowest socio-economic classes.
- It is not known whether schizophrenia causes an individual to drift into inner

city areas or whether the stress of living in such areas may trigger schizophrenia.

- Schizophrenic patients returning home from hospital are more likely to relapse if they live in families with high levels of negative EE.

- High levels of EE do not cause schizophrenia but may be a crucial factor in relapse prevention.

 (a) One behavioural therapy is the token economy system.

- Used with institutionalised patients based on operant conditioning.

- Patients are given tokens for desirable behaviours (e.g. self hygiene) which can be swapped for chocolates, cigarettes, etc., as positive reinforcers.

(b) The therapy can be evaluated in terms of effectiveness – does it work? – and ethics.

- Within the institution the therapy seems to work, but it is not so effective once the patient leaves the institution.

- Some argue that token economies are unethical because they restrict access to resources.

 There are many factors that affect eyewitness memory including the use of leading questions. Because you are asked to 'discuss', you need to provide evaluation for research in the form of commentary such as criticism, support and limitations.

- Research by Loftus has shown that leading questions produce errors in eyewitness recall (see Loftus & Zanni, 1975).

- Suggests that eyewitness memory is prone to reconstruction when leading questions are used by police and lawyers.

- However, her studies were lab based and so may not apply to recall of real-life crimes.

- One real-life crime study showed that leading questions did not produce errors in memory recall (see Yuille & Cutshall, 1987).

 Remember you must cover two psychological theories. Because you are asked to 'discuss', you need to provide evaluation for these theories in the form of commentary such as criticism, support and limitations.

- According to the theory of reasoned action, children may start smoking because they believe that it is acceptable.

- Based on this principle, educational programmes try to establish conservative norms that smoking is not acceptable.

- According to the health belief model it is possible to reduce the risk of AIDS by emphasising risk and demonstrating behaviour to reduce risk.

**7** Although methodology questions do not generally require essay answers, you should still answer in continuous prose and not list answers.

(a) The type of therapy given, either cognitive therapy or antidepressant medication.

(b) After one year, patients given either cognitive therapy or antidepressant medication will show differing rates of success.

(c) Nominal data.

(d) The results show that the majority of patients given cognitive therapy were discharged from hospital, whereas only approximately 50 per cent of the patients given antidepressant medication were released. It seems that cognitive therapy is more effective long-term than antidepressant medication.

(e) A chi square test would be used because the level of data is nominal and the design is unrelated.

**8** Remember you must cover two ethical principles. Because you are asked to 'discuss', you need to provide evaluation for these approaches in the form of commentary such as criticism, support and limitations.

- In general it is not ethically correct to deceive participants over the nature of a study and any procedures involved.

- Some studies could not have taken place unless they had deceived participants because knowledge of the real aim or procedures would make the study unrealistic.

- Before taking part in a study, participants should give their informed consent, being informed of the aim of a study and any procedures involved.

- In covert observation, participants are studied without their consent. If participants knew they were being observed their behaviour would not be natural.